Mother-Daughter Movies

"*We've got to talk—let's go to a movie.*"

St. Martin's Griffin ≈ New York

Rosemary Rogers and Nell Rogers Michlin

WITH CHRISTINE ERNST BODE

Mother-Daughter Movies

101 FILMS TO SEE TOGETHER

www.stmartins.com

Design by Susan Walsh

Illustrations by Michael Storrings

ISBN 0-312-32054-X
EAN 978-0312-32054-6

First Edition: May 2004

10 9 8 7 6 5 4 3 2 1

FOR

Two Mothers—Rose Rogers and Kathleen McKeever

AND

Two Filmmakers—Robert Downey Sr. and Ralf Bode

Contents

xiii

Acknowledgments

Many thanks to Hope Dellon, Kris Kamikawa, Frank Weimann, Catherine Barbosa, Mark Lotto, Clarissa Lasky, Steve McFarland, Christian O'Toole, Anne Lundberg, Tracy McNeil, Kim Jefferson, Chelsea Reck, Spencer Michlin, Ashley Feinstein, Linda Stasi, Kate Reid, Laura Groppe, Leanne Coronel, and Jackye Tobar, and especially to David Fisher for coming up with the idea in the first place.

Preface

Nobody has a perfect mother. And despite what some pushy moms would have us believe, nobody has a perfect daughter, either. It's sometimes hard to communicate with each other, but what can you do? Sadly, they haven't come up with a twelve-step program or even a *Dummies' Guide* for us. Should we turn to Dr. Phil, psychotropic drugs, a hit man? No! Here's our solution: it's so simple, so obvious, so painless—the Movies!

We're a mother and a daughter who have been watching movies together for over twenty years, so we've seen how, at any age, they jump-start important discussions. Movies give us a language and reference points for personal and uncomfortable (read: sex) issues. More than sitcoms, soap operas, or reality TV, they offer a peek into life experiences that need to be talked about, topics such as Dad, drugs, divorce, and that House of Horrors—High School.

Use movies to step outside of your relationship with your mother or with your daughter. We've tried and it works. You may think your mother only enjoys movies where Meryl weeps or your daughter's idea of a serious actor is Freddie Prinze Jr., but there are loads of movies that you can watch and enjoy together. What's more, movies do us an invaluable service by bringing us toxic mothers and blood-sucking daughters, monsters who make us look good and allow us to turn to our mother or daughter and think, "She's not *that* bad. . . ."

Life is complicated, and the mother-daughter relationship is fraught, but relating through hand puppets in family therapy isn't our idea of a good time. It turns out your local video store offers a better (and altogether less touchy-feely) solution. The movies have it all—shame spirals, virginity (or lack thereof), boundary issues, and bad skin.

We don't get all self-helpy in this book, either. In fact, just for fun (and to write off our Hollywood books and subscription to *People*), we've gone beyond the movies' bonding potential to include behind-the-scene info, gossip, and updates. We even deconstruct each film, evaluating its Hankie Factor and that all-important Hunk Factor. Finally, anyone who's ever watched a steamy sex scene with her mother or daughter will owe us a debt of gratitude for our sensitive ranking, Squirming in Your Seat Watching a Sex Scene with Your Mother/Daughter.

It wasn't easy, but we managed to narrow our list down to about one hundred movies, which we divided into categories. We love every movie in the book but realize that some may not be appropriate for younger girls. When that's the case, we've dubbed those movies OTOs (Older Teens Only). A mom can't be too careful!

So the next time it looks as if you two are going to throw down, Crawford-style, and one or both of you is eyeing the closet full of wire hangers, pick up this guide instead and work through your problems cinematically. It'll be a lot less painful, we promise.

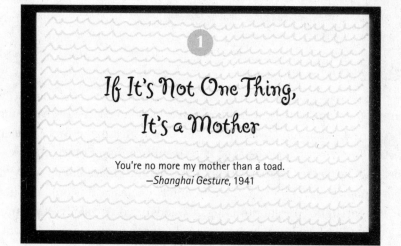

If It's Not One Thing, It's a Mother

You're no more my mother than a toad.
—Shanghai Gesture, 1941

Like it or not, we all have one. Even *your* mother had a mother who had a mother who—you get the point. Maybe your mom has turned passive aggression into an art form; maybe her idea of comfort food is a Lean Cuisine dinner; or, worse yet, maybe she insists on wearing culottes and a fanny pack in public. The following movies perform the invaluable service of reminding us that, as bad as we think we might have it, things could always be worse. One visit to our Nightmare Mom Hall of Fame and you'll be springing for the big basket of flowers next Mother's Day.

Ever After (1998)

Rated PG-13

Directed by Andy Tennant

Starring Drew Barrymore, Anjelica Huston, Dougray Scott, Megan Dodds, Melanie Lynskey, Jeroen Krabbé, Jeanne Moreau

THE PLOT

Ever After opens with a grande dame (Jeanne Moreau) giving the Brothers Grimm the lowdown on Cinderella. Her name was Danielle (Drew Barrymore) and she lived in sixteenth-century France. After the death of her father (Jeroen Krabbé), she had no choice but to live with her rather unsavory stepmother, Rodmilla (Anjelica Huston), and her two stepsisters, Marguerite (Megan Dodds) and Jacqueline (Melanie Lynskey). As if dealing with her beloved father's death weren't enough, her extended family has relegated her to the role of house servant.

One day Danielle meets Prince Henry (Dougray Scott), who's taken with her moxie and intelligence and begins to pursue her. Unfortunately, his parents—the king and queen of France—have Fancy Notions and want their son to marry a Spanish princess. Meanwhile, Rodmilla is suffering a serious cash flow problem, so she wants the prince to marry her daughter Marguerite. Love, as it will in fairy tales, conquers all. As the grande dame puts it, "And though Cinderella and her prince did live happily ever after, the point, gentlemen, is that they lived."

Here's a postfeminist Cinderella in Renaissance costumes—no pumpkins, no fairy godmother, no Bibbity Boppity Boo. As the ads announced, "This is not your grandmother's Cinderella." Indeed. Danielle is handy with a knife and sword and rescues *herself* from the mossy-toothed villain. On one occasion, she even saves Prince Henry's life. He's impressed:

Prince Henry: You swim alone, climb rocks, rescue servants. Is there anything you don't do?
Danielle: Fly!

Bonding Potential: 5

Any retelling of Cinderella should make young girls grateful for their moms, even when mom is insisting that they pick up their socks. We all need mother love, proactive fairy-tale heroines included. Danielle reaches out to Rodmilla:

> *Danielle*: You are the only mother I have ever known. Was there a time, even in its smallest measurement, that you loved me at all?
> *Rodmilla*: How can anyone love a pebble in their shoe?

Tell us how you *really* feel, Rodmilla!

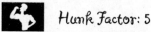 Hunk Factor: 5

3

Dougray Scott does not disappoint as a dashing prince. Though, at the risk of sounding indelicate, we have to say it looks as if he's stuffed a loin of pork down his tights. We're dealing with a PG-13 movie, after all. (This might, however, explain why he was cast in *Another 9½ Weeks*.)

 Hankie Factor: 0

Squirming in Your Seat Watching a Sex Scene with Your Mother/Daughter Factor: 0

BEHIND THE SCENES

The Cinderella story, originating in China, now exists in at least five hundred different versions. Director Tennant said about his treatment, "I have two daughters. I did not want them growing up believing you have to marry a rich guy with a big house to live happily ever after."

AFTERMATH

The real Prince Henry of France married the decidedly un-Cinderella-like Catherine de Médicis, whose real-life antics far surpassed anything Rodmilla could have dreamed up.

Mommie Dearest (1981)
Rated PG

Directed by Frank Perry
Starring Faye Dunaway, Diana Scarwid, Mara Hobel, Steve Forrest

THE PLOT

4

With her career on the fritz and several flop marriages under her belt, movie star Joan Crawford (Faye Dunaway) decides to adopt some children. The kids provide plenty of photo ops, but get in the way of Joan's beauty sleep, sex life, and anal retention. Christina (Mara Hobel/Diana Scarwid) bears the brunt of Joan's wrath, especially when Mom spots some much despised wire hangers in her closet. Mama Crawford continues to abuse Christina, physically and mentally, until she finally sends her away to boarding school. When Joan dies, she stiffs Christina in her will, so her daughter exacts revenge by writing her book, *Mommie Dearest*.

Movies like *Mostly Martha* and *About a Boy* would have us believe that adopted kids bring redemption and meaning to an adult's life. Well, it sure didn't work that way for Joan Crawford. Her famously brutish battles with her daughter brought the world her deliciously quotable war cries "No wire hangers—ever!" and "Tina! Bring me the ax!" This is how Crawford, the former queen of MGM, is remembered today. Does this mean future generations will never see her dancing in blackface in *Torch Song*?

This film makes an excellent double feature with *Mildred Pierce*, which has Joan as the long-suffering mom, Mildred. In *Mommie*

Dearest, we see Joan as she rehearses for the *Mildred Pierce* audition and wins an Oscar for the role.

💛 Bonding Potential: 8

All mothers owe Joan Crawford a debt of gratitude. We all lose it at some time or another, as when we suspect our sloppy daughters just might be growing subspecies under their beds. But do we pummel our daughters with Ajax the way Joan does? No. She's not exactly a good sport, either. She challenges young Christina to a swimming race and handily wins.

> *Christina:* You're bigger than me. It's not fair.
> *Joan:* Ah, but no one ever said life was fair, Tina. I'm bigger and faster. I'll always beat you.

Any mom who lets her 5-year-old win at Candy Land should feel pretty darn good about herself.

5

💪 Hunk Factor: 0

There are no hunks to speak of, though Joan does exude a pretty masculine vibe.

Hankie Factor: 0

 Squirming in Your Seat Watching a Sex Scene with Your Mother/Daughter Factor: 0

BEHIND THE SCENES

Christina Crawford hated this adaptation of her book, beefing, "They made it into a Joan Crawford movie!" Faye Dunaway also hated it, as well she should: Many people believe that her over-the-top performance ruined her career.

AFTERMATH

The movie did poorly at the box office, won the Razzie Award for the Worst Picture of the Year, but went on to be a camp classic. Campiness aside, the movie *Mommie Dearest* and the book (which sold 4 million copies) did much to raise public awareness of child abuse.

Now, Voyager (1942)

Not Rated

Directed by Irving Rapper
Starring Bette Davis, Claude Rains, Paul Henreid, Gladys Cooper, John Loder

6

THE PLOT

Repressed Charlotte Vale (Bette Davis), of the repressed Boston Vales, lives in a mansion with her repressed and repressive mother (Gladys Cooper). Charlotte is the family old maid: she's fat, bushy-browed, and an emotional basket case, despite Mother's insistence that "no member of the Vale family has ever had a nervous breakdown!" Charlotte is sent to Cascade, a gorgeous sanitarium where a kindly psychiatrist, Dr. Jacquith (Claude Rains), nurses her back to health. She loses a lot of weight, plucks her eyebrows, trades her support hose in for some nylons, and takes a South American cruise. (Hey, do they have a bed available at Cascade?) While traipsing around South America, she meets Jerry (Paul Henreid) and the two fall in love, but unfortunately Jerry is married to a controlling hypochondriac. Back in Boston, Charlotte receives a marriage proposal from a wealthy widower, Elliot Livingstone (John Loder). She quarrels with Mother, who promptly dies, forcing Charlotte back to the sanitarium for a tune-up. While there, she meets an adolescent girl, Tina, with whom Charlotte immediately identifies. It turns out that Tina is Jerry's daughter, and her emotional problems stem from a troubled relationship with *her* mother, the aforementioned hypochondriac.

In the beginning of the movie we find out that Charlotte hides lots of things from her miserable mother, including the fact that she smokes. Ironic, considering how Bette Davis was, and still is, the screen's greatest cigarette smoker. The most memorable scene in *Now, Voyager* is when Jerry lights two cigarettes and then gives one to Charlotte. It's always a big moment for them (and us) when that happens.

 ## Bonding Potential: 8

The two mothers of *Now, Voyager* are best summarized as "tyranny masquerading as mother love." Early on, Charlotte tells Dr. Jacquith: "I'm fat. My mother doesn't approve of dieting. Look at my shoes. My mother approves of sensible shoes. Look at the books on my shelves. My mother approves of good solid books. I'm my mother's well-loved daughter. I'm her companion. I am my mother's servant. My mother says! My mother! My mother! *My mother*!" Who wouldn't have a nervous breakdown? When Charlotte and Tina connect, they find in each other the maternal bond they both need and deserve.

Hunk Factor: 2

Paul Henreid has never been a favorite of ours. We would have stayed in Casablanca with Rick, and frankly, we would have married Elliot Livingstone.

Hankie Factor: 6

Now, Voyager is what used to be referred to as a woman's weepie. Just try to stay dry-eyed when Charlotte says, "You see, no one ever called me *darling* before," or "Oh, Jerry, why ask for the moon when we already have the stars?"

P.S. *Why* couldn't they have had both the moon and the stars? They had divorce back in 1942. But then this would be a hankie-free movie.

Squirming in Your Seat Watching a Sex Scene with Your Mother/Daughter Factor: 0

BEHIND THE SCENES

Paul Henreid invented that bit about lighting the two cigarettes. Nonetheless, his career went downhill after *Now, Voyager.* His final screen appearance was in *Exorcist II: The Heretic,* pound-for-pound the worst movie ever made. Bette Davis proposed a different ending for the movie: She wanted Charlotte to run off with Dr. Jacquith.

AFTERMATH

The title and theme come from Walt Whitman's *Leaves of Grass,* the same opus that Monica Lewinsky once gave President Bill Clinton.

Postcards from the Edge (1990)

Rated R

Directed by Mike Nichols
Starring Meryl Streep, Shirley MacLaine, Dennis Quaid, Gene Hackman, Richard Dreyfuss, Rob Reiner

THE PLOT

Suzanne (Meryl Streep) has hit rock bottom before the opening credits even roll. The pill-popping, coke-addled, binge-drinking actress has been thrown off the set of her latest movie, passes out in some strange guy's bed, and winds up in the hospital with her stomach pumped. Which is the least of her problems: Upon release from rehab, she finds herself living back at her mom's house. Her mom (Shirley MacLaine), an actress even more famous than Suzanne, may be a celebrated performer, but she never really mastered the role of mother.

Though *Postcards from the Edge* has much to say, funny and sad, about Hollywood, addiction, and recovery, the film is increasingly concerned with the complicated and melodramatic relationship be-

DISSING MOM

"It's a terrible thing to hate your mother. But I didn't always hate her. When I was a child, I only kind of disliked her."
—LAURENCE HARVEY, *The Manchurian Candidate*

"Mother—what is the phrase?—isn't quite herself today."
—ANTHONY PERKINS, *Psycho*

"You're not a mother, you're a telephone operator."
—HENRY THOMAS, *Raggedy Man*

"My mother should have raised cobras, not children."
—NICK NOLTE, *The Prince of Tides*

"I had one of those mothers who was always telling people her daughter was her best friend. When she said it, I'd think, 'Great—not only do I have a shitty mother, my best friend is a loser bitch.'"
—CHRISTINA RICCI, *The Opposite of Sex*

"Your mother did it to you, and her mother did it to her—back to Eve."
—GENE HACKMAN, *Postcards from the Edge*

"Fun-sucker!"
—LINDSAY LOHAN, *Freaky Friday*

9

tween Suzanne and her mother. Based on Carrie Fisher's eponymous novel (which draws on her own troubles with drugs and real-life mom Debbie Reynolds), the film is a lot of witty thrust and parry between two great actresses, Meryl Streep and Shirley MacLaine. The script has a vicious barbed wit, and when these two aren't throwing words like serrated knives, they talk over and past each other. This is every mother-daughter relationship multiplied by a hundred.

Bonding Potential: 10

If you think you have a nutty relationship with your mother/daughter, you'll feel like Jo and Marmee compared with Suzanne and Doris. Evidently, a coddled, narcissistic movie star does not a nurturing mother make; Doris is by turns self-centered, arrogant, and insincere. The aging performer, haunted by her falling star, uses her daughter's recovery as an opportunity to control her comings and goings, to offer unsolicited advice, and to generally relive her own experiences as a Hollywood ingenue. Suzanne rolls her eyes like an embarrassed teenager and seeks refuge in sarcasm. Streep deploys her considerable talents to portray Suzanne as a delicate, angry, confused, and desperate woman barely holding it together. It takes a crisis to unite them, humbling Doris and forcing Suzanne to grow up and take responsibility for her life. If those two can work toward a resolution, mothers and daughters the world over should be able to coexist in harmony.

Hunk Factor: 7

Dennis Quaid works his trademark grin as Jack, a Hollywood lothario who seduces Suzanne. His arsenal of come-ons includes gems like "Did anyone tell you, you smell like the future?" Somehow, he makes it work.

Hankie Factor: 3

This film might strike a nerve if you're a member of a dysfunctional Hollywood dynasty, but otherwise expect your eyes to remain dry.

Squirming in Your Seat Watching a Sex Scene with Your Mother/Daughter Factor: 3

Suzanne winds up in bed with a strange man. Never a good moment.

BEHIND THE SCENES

The framed poster in Doris's house of Doris and a young Suzanne on the cover of *Life* magazine is a real cover shot of Shirley MacLaine and her daughter.

AFTERMATH

Carrie Fisher reentered drug rehab in 1998. Some time after that, she revealed that she suffers from bipolar disorder.

Real Women Have Curves (2002)
Rated PG-13

Directed by Patricia Cardoso
Starring America Ferrara, Lupe Ontiveros, Ingrid Oliu, George Lopez, Brian Sites, Soledad St. Hilaire

THE PLOT

This coming-of-age story focuses on a strong-willed first-generation American girl, Ana (America Ferrara), caught between two cultures.

11

Her equally stubborn mother, Carmen (Lupe Ontiveros), believes there is some virtue in the tradition of leading a difficult life. Ana's less feisty older sister, Estella (Ingrid Oliu), lives at home and owns a small sewing factory nearby in the mostly Hispanic Boyle Heights neighborhood in East Los Angeles. Upon finishing high school, Ana goes to work with her sister, and comes to realize that Estella's life is more difficult and complicated than she had initially thought.

When Ana's teacher, Mr. Guzman (George Lopez), comes to her house to inform her that she has been accepted at Columbia University with a full scholarship, Ana's life is turned upside down. Her traditional parents want to keep the family geographically connected, and in Carmen's mind it is absolutely out of the question for Ana to move across the country to get an education. They are afraid that the family will be broken up, or worse, that Ana will become a different person.

For years, Carmen has told Ana that she is fat, yet the self-secure teenager doesn't believe that she is unattractive. "You're not bad looking, just fat. If you lost weight you would be so beautiful." Ana is having none of it: "There's so much more to me than what I weigh." We can empathize with all of the characters in this movie, but particularly with Carmen and Ana. It's clear that they love each other, but fear and pride get in their way, making it difficult for them to communicate honestly with each other.

Bonding Potential: 10

This mother-daughter relationship is complex and will provide fodder for hours of conversation. Carmen has imported her traditional views from the old country—views about marriage and children—which she tries to impose on Ana. Yet it is clear that Ana is an American girl; she wants to be independent and educated and recognized for her intelligence. They have seemingly irreconcilable conflicts, but ones that any mother and daughter can relate to.

Real Women Have Curves is not a cornball boost to big girls who insist they're happy just as they are. This is a sweet, amusing ode to daughters and mothers, and a refreshing homage to real women.

Most of us do not look like waifish models and actresses; just go into any store dressing room for proof. Ana is a real young woman, and she is beautiful.

 Hunk Factor: 0

Nada.

 Hankie Factor: 0

No es necesario.

Squirming in Your Seat Watching a Sex Scene with Your Mother/Daughter Factor: 2

13

Ana loses her virginity in a perfunctory "Let's get it over with" kind of way. She likes the guy and he likes her, but she isn't looking for Prince Charming, and shortly after the event, he leaves for college.

BEHIND THE SCENES

All the money people (until HBO) wanted white women to play Hispanic, bankable stars, and skinny women in fat suits. The casting calls said "no skinny girls," and lots of skinny girls who thought they were fat showed up.

AFTERMATH

When *Real Women Have Curves* premiered at the 2002 Sundance Film Festival, the audience went wild, giving it the Dramatic Audience Award as well as a Special Acting Prize for its costars, Lupe Ontiveros and America Ferrara.

Riding in Cars with Boys (2001)

Rated PG-13

Directed by Penny Marshall

Starring Drew Barrymore, Steve Zahn, Brittany Murphy, Lorraine Bracco, James Woods, Adam Garcia, Rosie Perez

THE PLOT

Viewers may be surprised to discover that *Riding in Cars with Boys,* the true story of Beverly Donofrio, a mother at fifteen, is based on a memoir by Beverly and not by her son Jason. It could just as easily be entitled *The Case Against My Mother.* With Penny Marshall at the helm and bad-girl-made-good Drew Barrymore playing Beverly, we might have expected a fairy tale about some cute, irrepressible single mom who triumphs against all odds. What we get instead is the bitterly funny story of a girl who is too young, too smart, too selfish, and too self-pitying to really care for anyone besides herself.

But Beverly's not a bad mom exactly, and you'd have to be Pat Robertson not to feel for her. After all, she's a child with a child, married to a deadbeat junkie, living in absolute squalor, her dreams of leaving sixties-era small-town Connecticut for New York, of going to college, of becoming a writer, all but extinguished. Then again, she constantly heaps all the blame on her young son—in actual fact, the only blameless one here—raising Jason to believe that he's just an anchor around her neck. That he mothers her more often than she does him, Beverly seems to think only fair.

Barrymore ages twenty years over the course of two hours—the layers of makeup are not so convincing, but they are thankfully not too distracting—and she gives a courageous performance as a woman both compellingly sympathetic and entirely unlikable. Steve Zahn, as her hapless, strung-out husband Ray, is all at once sweet, funny, and heartbreaking; his unique comic timing, always that half-step late, is used here to create a father and a husband who is eager to please but dangerously unreliable.

14

Bonding Potential: 6

Despite what *The Gilmore Girls* might have you believe, teen parenting isn't always fun and easy, particularly for an aspiring writer who is ambitious, naive, and exceptionally self-involved, even for a teenager. And Beverly's parents, shamed by their daughter's scandalous behavior, don't exactly give her the emotional support that she needs. Mom (Lorraine Bracco) channels whatever maternal energy she possesses into cleaning, while Dad (James Woods) seems to have graduated first in his class from the Tough Love School of Parenting. So Beverly, refusing to give up on her curtailed dreams, raises Jason with equal parts love and resentment. Perhaps the film's finest accomplishment is the way it captures Beverly as both selfish and forgivable. The result is that viewers will simultaneously feel for her and breathe a sigh of relief that she's not their mother (or daughter, for that matter).

 Hunk Factor: 4

The cutest guy in the movie is Adam Garcia (*Coyote Ugly*), who plays the 20-year-old Jason. Zahn, who has mastered the art of the lovable goof, is charming despite his considerable problems, which is no easy feat.

 Hankie Factor: 3

Beverly's best girlfriend, Fay (Brittany Murphy), is touchingly devoted and fiercely protective, and her speech at Beverly's shotgun wedding might cause some eyes to well up. Also, Kleenex may be required for the film's last ten minutes. There is reconciliation all around: Beverly and her son, Jason and his father, Beverly and her father.

The sex scenes are classic early sixties make-out scenes. It's hard to believe that Beverly and Fay got pregnant as a result of these fetid

16

FILL IN THE BLANKS

"I fart in your general direction. Your mother was a _____."
    —JOHN CLEESE, *Monty Python and the Holy Grail*
Answer: *hamster*

"That's the trouble with mothers. You get to like them and they _____."
    —KAY FRANCIS, *Trouble in Paradise*
Answer: *die*

"It's all part of your contempt for the family unit. You think *mother* is a
_____ _____."
    —ANGELA LANSBURY, *All Fall Down*
Answer: *dirty word*

"All I ever had was _____."
    —JAMES CAGNEY, *White Heat*
Answer: *Ma*

"My mother's away for Christmas. She's spending it at the _____
_____."
    —JONATHAN PRYCE, *Brazil*
Answer: *plastic surgeon*

adolescent couplings. Any squirming would more likely be a result of the over-cutesy kid actors.

BEHIND THE SCENES

The real Beverly and the real Jason make cameo appearances in the movie, sitting behind Drew Barrymore in the wedding scene. Barrymore must have found elements of her own life in the story of a survivor who married a drunk and a drug addict. She is descended from generations of similarly afflicted thespians and has struggled with her own substance abuse.

AFTERMATH

Beverly was involved in the making of the movie, which was marked by tension between the director, Penny Marshall, and the producer, James Brooks. Jason, who objected to his fictional love interest, married his real girlfriend after the movie was released.

17

White Oleander (2002)

Rated PG-13

Directed by Peter Kosminsky
Starring Michelle Pfeiffer, Alison Lohman, Renée Zellweger, Robin Wright Penn,
Svetlana Efremova, Billy Connelly

THE PLOT

Astrid Magnussen (Alison Lohman), 15, lives with her artist mother, Ingrid (Michelle Pfeiffer), in California. She adores her mother and their life together is happy, if unorthodox, until Ingrid is unceremoniously dumped by her boyfriend, Barry (Billy Connelly). Not one to take rejection lightly, Ingrid murders him with her favorite flower, a white oleander, which like her is beautiful and poisonous. She is sentenced to thirty-five years in prison and Astrid is sentenced to foster homes and foster mothers (Robin Wright Penn, Renée Zellweger, Svetlana Efremova). The movie tracks Astrid's life as she moves from home to home while her mother, a master of manipulation, controls her every move from within prison.

Astrid worships her mom, but understands that she is dangerous. Among other things, *White Oleander* is about a daughter trying to get away from a Toxic Mom. Ingrid warns her, "Stay away from broken people," curious advice coming from a woman who killed her boyfriend because he didn't call, didn't write.

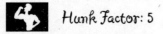 Bonding Potential: 8

We know right away that Ingrid isn't exactly June Cleaver when she passes on Parents' Night with the comment "What can they tell me about you that I don't already know?" Nice try, Ingrid, but we all have to go to Parents' Night, and why should you be spared? Her idea of uplifting maternal advice is this bon mot: "Love humiliates you, but hate cradles you." Just in case you have any doubt of the influence mothers have on their daughters, look at Ingrid and Astrid: Mom consumes her daughter, telling her, "I am in your blood." No wonder the movie's tagline is "Where does a mother end and a daughter begin?"

 Hunk Factor: 5

Did we mention Ray, the boyfriend of Astrid's first foster mom? He's played by Cole Hauser, a serious looker.

Hankie Factor: 2

The first time Ingrid sees her mother after she's been in prison, she breaks down, and we felt like crying, too. Mom breaks the mood, telling Astrid not to cry because "We're Vikings." Huh?

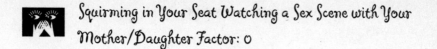
BEHIND THE SCENES

It looked to us as though Michelle Pfeiffer had pricey highlights throughout the entire movie, even when her character was supposedly molting in prison.

The book *White Oleander* by Janet Fitch became famous when it was made an Oprah Book Club selection. Its many fans insist you should read the book before seeing the movie. We didn't, and we're fine with that.

AFTERMATH

In an interview, Michelle flatly stated that the character of Astrid "baffled me . . . however destructive, narcissistic, selfish, and annihilating she might be, she is also very truthful and I think there is a lot of truth to what she says." Michelle went on to assure us that in real life, she's a good mother. Alison Lohman went on to steal a movie from Nic Cage, 2003's *Matchstick Men*.

19

American Beauty (1999)
Rated R

Directed by Sam Mendes
Starring Kevin Spacey, Annette Bening, Thora Birch, Mena Suvari, Chris Cooper,
Allison Janney, Wes Bentley, Peter Gallagher

THE PLOT

20

The members of the Burnham family, Lester (Kevin Spacey), Carolyn (Annette Bening), and daughter Jane (Thora Birch), lead separate lives under the same roof. Carolyn, a high-strung real estate agent, is smitten with her boss (Peter Gallagher). Lester, after becoming obsessed with his daughter's cheerleader friend (Mena Suvari), quits his job, starts smoking pot, and commences an intense weight lifting regimen. In short he tunes in, turns on, and works out. In the meantime, an equally dysfunctional family (Chris Cooper, Allison Janney) moves in next door and Jane connects with their son Ricky (Wes Bentley).

Lester embodies a life of quiet desperation. The movie opens with him telling the audience, "Both my wife and daughter think I'm this gigantic loser. And they're right." And just as Lester goes on a journey of self-realization and redemption, so does his daughter. *American Beauty* gives us insight into several representatives of the male species and never dissolves into cliché: man in a midlife crisis; homophobic abuser; sensitive young man; ambitious boss; homosexuals, latent and decidedly un-so.

♥♥ Bonding Potential: 6

While Jane is a typical teenager, sulky and uncommunicative, Carolyn is *not* a typical mother. She is the Anti-Mother: narcissistic, on the edge, incapable of nurturing. Her fixation with appearances extends even to having her gardening shears match her gardening clogs. She asks her daughter, "Are you *trying* to look unattractive?" When Jane responds affirmatively, Carolyn says, "Congratulations, you succeeded admirably." Hey, take it easy, Carolyn. Worst of all, when driving alone in her car, she is either listening to self-help tapes or singing along with snappy, sappy show tunes, most notably "Don't Rain on My Parade."

Hunk Factor: 6

Wes Bentley is sensitive and brooding, the perfect teenage lust object.

HUNKS FOR MOM

1. Ralph Fiennes, *The English Patient*

2. Mel Gibson, *The Year of Living Dangerously*

3. James Dean, *Giant*

4. Albert Finney, *Tom Jones*

5. Denzel Washington, *Devil in a Blue Dress*

6. Robert De Niro, *The Deer Hunter*

7. Ewan McGregor, *Moulin Rouge*

8. Daniel Day-Lewis, *The Age of Innocence*

9. Laurence Olivier, *Wuthering Heights*

10. Antonio Banderas, *Tie Me Up, Tie Me Down*

Hankie Factor: 0

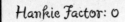 Squirming in Your Seat Watching a Sex Scene with Your Mother/Daughter Factor: 8

There are several fantasy scenes that could get uncomfortable, but when Lester and Angela get intimate, it's uncomfortable for everyone: mothers, daughters, household pets, and lawn ornaments alike. Even if he *has* been lifting weights, a middle-aged lothario should not be kissing a young teenager—it's unsightly, uncomfortable, and a defining squirm moment.

BEHIND THE SCENES

Mendes, in this directorial debut, watched *Sunset Boulevard, The Apartment, Ordinary People*, even *Marathon Man* for inspiration. Paula Abdul choreographed the cheerleading scene where Lester first sees Angela. The original script had Ricky and Jane arrested and standing trial for Lester's murder.

AFTERMATH

Kevin Spacey won an Academy Award for his performance.

22

Like Water for Chocolate (1993)

Rated R

Directed by Alfonso Arau

Starring Lumi Cavazos, Marco Leonardi, Regina Torné, Mario Iván Martinez, Ada Carrasco, Yareli Arizmenti, Claudette Maillé

THE PLOT

Tita (Lumi Cavazos) is the last daughter in a family that adheres to the Mexican custom that requires the youngest daughter to live at home with her mother until her death. This is bad news for Pedro (Marco Leonardi), who asks Mamá Elena (Regina Torné) for Tita's hand. As a consolation prize, she offers instead her eldest daughter, Rosaura (Yareli Arizmenti), which causes middle sister Gertrudis (Claudette Maillé) to shriek, "You can't just exchange tacos for enchiladas!" Pedro accepts Rosaura so he can be near Tita, who is equally smitten. She spends most of her time in the kitchen with the cook, Nacha (Ada Carrasco), creating elaborate and supernaturally charmed dishes that move people to joy, sorrow, lust, and even mortal flatulence.

Too bad Tita couldn't have put her mother in a nursing home. Though we feel for her, not being able to marry the man she loves and all, we wish she'd stopped lusting after him once he became her brother-in-law. Still, it's heartwarming to see their love withstand time, revolutions, and a really mean mom. *Like Water for Chocolate* is a very sensuous story about the power and magic of love. *Warning*: Have some take-out menus handy, because this is one of those movies, like *Chocolat*, that make you *very* hungry.

 Bonding Potential: 6

Mamá Elena is so bad, she makes Joan Crawford look good. Thankfully, Tita gets some much needed mother love (not to mention yummy cooking tips) from Nacha. And this dutiful daughter gets her

23

revenge at the end of the movie when she exorcises her hideous mother (in spirit form) from her life forever.

 Hunk Factor: 2

Pedro is hunky in that short, dark, and handsome way.

Hankie Factor: 3

When a suitor, Doctor John (Mario Iván Martinez), professes his true love for Tita, it is the first time she's ever experienced this kind of selflessness. Face it: Unconditional love is always hankie-inducing.

Squirming in Your Seat Watching a Sex Scene with Your Mother/Daughter Factor: 8

In Mexico, hot chocolate is made by combining chocolate and boiling water. This culinary practice inspired the adage "Like water for chocolate," which denotes that someone is extremely sexually aroused. We see this idiom brought to life during one very steamy (but fabulously romantic) sex scene, which features both male and female full frontal nudity.

BEHIND THE SCENES

Director Arau was married at the time to Laura Esquivel, who wrote the best-selling book as well as the screenplay for this movie.

AFTERMATH

This movie cleaned up at Mexico's Ariel Awards, winning eleven in total.

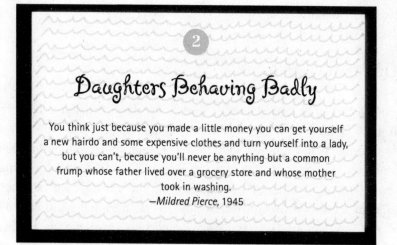

2

Daughters Behaving Badly

You think just because you made a little money you can get yourself
a new hairdo and some expensive clothes and turn yourself into a lady,
but you can't, because you'll never be anything but a common
frump whose father lived over a grocery store and whose mother
took in washing.
—*Mildred Pierce*, 1945

Who spawned these feral beasts, anyhow? Why have they turned on their mother, the person who loves them most of all? Changing all those diapers, getting them ready for school, listening to Justin Timberlake—doesn't that count for anything? No, it doesn't, and thankfully, you didn't become a mom for the great salary or the constant words of gratitude you receive. Feel better by checking out some of these psycho demon daughters.

Freaky Friday (2003)

Rated PG

Directed by Mark S. Waters

Starring Jamie Lee Curtis, Lindsay Lohan, Mark Harmon, Harold Gould, Chad Michael
Murray

THE PLOT

Freaky Friday begins as mother Tess (Jamie Lee Curtis) and daughter
Anna (Lindsay Lohan) seem to have reached an impasse. The viewer
has trouble believing the two are even related, much less mother and
daughter (so do they). Tall, lanky, brunette Tess, a widowed psychiatrist about to be remarried, juggles her frantic schedule with the help
of what seems like an entire Best Buy's worth of cellular and PDA de-
vices. Tiny blonde Anna is otherwise occupied with failing English
and falling in like with motorcycle-riding Jake (Chad Michael Murray), but plays a mean guitar in her garage band. We are made to
believe that Anna is rebelling in a rather harmless, Disneyfied alterni-
teen sort of way, the chunky streaks in her hair and pierced navel in-
dicating angst. She also fights with her mother constantly, Anna
shouting her adolescent war cry "You're ruining my life!" while Tess
spouts annoying psychobabble. And then, magically, they switch bodies on a monumentally busy Friday, chock-full of big tests, TV appearances, band auditions, and wedding rehearsal dinners. Comedy, and
ultimately communication, ensues.

There's a reason why *Freaky Friday,* the eponymous 1972 novel
upon which it was based, and the 1976 original film version are all so
popular: The story brings to life an age-old fantasy of mothers and
daughters the world over. And sure enough, challenges like "You
couldn't last a day in my shoes!" have launched many a body-
swapping comedy. Of course we're expected to suspend disbelief as
the impossible unfolds, but there is nevertheless something true at
work in these switcheroo comedies. At times humans, perhaps none
more so than mothers and their teenage daughters, seem to need

26

something along the lines of a miracle, even a momentary lapse in the time-space continuum, in order to understand one another.

 ## Bonding Potential: 10

If ever a movie were made to bring mothers and daughters closer together, *Freaky Friday* is it. Anna and Tess are two aggressively dissimilar people who, on opposite sides of a canyon-sized generation gap, can't seem to see each other clearly. Switching places finally allows each of them to understand what the other is going through. It's widely accepted that parents and teenagers, though they might inhabit the same dwelling, can be near-strangers. This movie plays on the idea that these "strangers" have a great deal to learn about each other. Sure enough, the more time Anna spends in her mother's body, the more respect and admiration she has for all that her mother has accomplished. And the longer Tess masquerades as her daughter, the more she is able to appreciate how difficult her life can be. In the end, they come to accept each other and celebrate their differences, rather than letting those differences alienate them.

 ## Hunk Factor: 7

Chad Michael Murray, the WB's resident teen heartthrob, here scruffs it up to play the nonthreatening bad boy Jake. He's pretty appealing, especially as he's trying to convince Anna-as-Tess that she should indulge in a May–December romance. Mark Harmon is less charming as Tess's pushover fiancé.

Hankie Factor: 6

Freaky Friday provides a lot of laughs, but has its touching moments, too. At the rehearsal dinner, it becomes evident that Anna is still trying to come to terms with her father's death. In Tess's body, she makes a teary toast in which she muses, "It's great we're getting married—even though my husband died. How quickly I've been able to get over it." We see her pain and confusion, and so, finally, does her mother.

Squirming in Your Seat Watching a Sex Scene with Your Mother/Daughter Factor: 3

When Tess's fiancé, unaware of the mother-daughter switcheroo, tries to put the moves on Anna-as-Tess, the movie becomes a touch squirmy. But not too much so—it's Disney, after all.

BEHIND THE SCENES

Jodie Foster, who played the Anna role in the 1976 original, turned down the role of Tess because she felt that it might overshadow the movie.

AFTERMATH

Jamie Lee Curtis won rave reviews for her comedic turn as Tess; Lindsay Lohan, who also starred in Disney's remake of *The Parent Trap* in 1998, sealed her fate as a tween superstar.

Imitation of Life (1959)

Rated PG

Directed by Douglas Sirk

Starring Lana Turner, John Gavin, Sandra Dee, Susan Kohner, Juanita Moore, Troy
 Donahue

THE PLOT

Wannabe actress Lora Meredith (Lana Turner) takes in a fellow struggling single mom, Annie (Juanita Moore), who just happens to be
black. The two women and their daughters merge their lives together,
with Annie taking the role of domestic servant. Ten years later, Lora's
showbiz success has destroyed her relationships with both her
daughter Susie (Sandra Dee) and boyfriend Steve (John Gavin). Annie
has problems of her own: her light-skinned daughter, Sarah Jane
(Susan Kohner), is passing for white, and in the process, totally trash-
ing her sainted mother.

29

It should be pointed out that, despite the "colored girl" references,
Imitation of Life was, for its time, incredibly progressive. Few films of
that era—lavish color melodramas least of all—dealt with racial prejudice. What *was* shocking about the movie, however, was how it ex-
ploited the tabloid woes of its leading lady, Lana Turner. Prior to
filming, Lana's teenage daughter, Cheryl, killed Mom's gangster
boyfriend, Johnny Stompanato, with a butcher knife. This scandal
grew to O.J. Simpson proportions. The movie's soap opera plot re-
sembled the star's soap opera reality (imitation of life?), a fact not lost
on Universal's publicity department. Not surprisingly, *Imitation of
Life* was its biggest moneymaker that year.

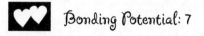 Bonding Potential: 7

Daughters are always embarrassed by their mothers at one time
or another. Sarah Jane's desire to "pass" results in her cruel rejection

of her mother: "*I* don't want to have to come through back doors or feel lower than other people or apologize for my mother's color. She can't help her color, but I can and will. I want to have a chance in life." The only one who isn't imitating life is Annie, who moans, "It's a sin to be ashamed of what you are—and it's a sin to lie about who you are."

Working mothers are always torn between their jobs and their kids. Lora Meredith's ambition ("I'm going up and up and up!") causes her to neglect her daughter Susie and ignore the racial tragedy in her own home. The movie clearly holds to the 1950s point of view that you can't be a mother *and* have a career. Good guy Steve finally gives Lora the ultimatum: him or showbiz. Didn't he ever hear of a two-income family? And as if their relationship wasn't strained enough, Susie grows up to vie with Mom for Steve (shades of *Mildred Pierce and* Johnny Stompanato).

30

 Hunk Factor: 1

John Gavin is a big stiff who seems to have a mixture of shoe polish and KY Jelly in his hair. This movie introduced the big-time hunk of the early 1960s, Troy Donahue.

 Hankie Factor: 10

This is an unrepentant tearjerker. Okay, so younger moviegoers might not be moved by Mahalia Jackson's spiritual "Trouble of the World" at the end of the movie. But they should be.

Squirming in Your Seat Watching a Sex Scene with Your Mother/Daughter Factor: 0

BEHIND THE SCENES

A white actress, Susan Kohner, played the role of African-American Sarah Jane. Kohner might have been the wrong race, but she did win an Academy Award nomination. She was the daughter of Lana Turner's agent, and is mother to the directors of *About a Boy*.

AFTERMATH

The money she earned from this movie, which capitalized on her personal scandal, kept Lana Turner solvent for the rest of her messy life. She married and divorced several more times; her last husband was a sleazy magician who did a disappearing act with all her jewelry. Screen daughter Sandra Dee, a stand-in for all the goody-goody girls of the sixties, went on to grapple with bulimia and booze. Lana's real-life daughter, Cheryl Crane, finally found happiness with galpal Josh (née Joyce) LeRoy. The two were at Lana's side when she died.

31

Mildred Pierce (1945)
Not rated

Directed by Michael Curtiz
Starring Joan Crawford, Ann Blyth, Zachary Scott, Eve Arden, Jack Carson,
    Bruce Bennett.

THE PLOT

Working single mom Mildred Pierce (Joan Crawford) sacrifices all for her spoiled daughter, Veda (Ann Blyth). After Mildred kicks her faithless husband (Bruce Bennett) to the curb, the plucky mom parleys a waitress job into a successful business with the help of Ida (Eve Arden) and Wally (Jack Carson). In a desperate attempt to placate the venal Veda, Mildred marries penniless playboy Monte Beragon (Zachary Scott), and from there, the story gets really messy.

It's our firm belief that every responsible mother is obligated to introduce her daughter to old black-and-white movies, particularly film noir classics. *Mildred Pierce* is the prototypical woman's picture. There's murder, sex (mother and daughter share a lover), scotch on the rocks, feigned pregnancy, hootchy-kootchy dancing, and ankle-strap high heels, which at the time were vulgarly referred to as "Joan Crawford-fuck-me-fast shoes."

 Bonding Potential: 7

Veda is such a nightmare that she inspires Ida to crack the memorable line "Personally, I think alligators have the right idea. They eat their young." As far as we can tell, there's nothing wrong with the long-suffering Mildred, but her daughter finds her repulsive and even accuses her of "smelling like chicken."

 Hunk Factor: 0

One of Mildred's admirers sweats a lot, another looks like a pimp in an ascot, and her ex-husband is a nose talker.

Hankie Factor: 2

Mildred tries, but cannot find happiness.

Squirming in Your Seat Watching a Sex Scene with Your Mother/Daughter Factor: 0

BEHIND THE SCENES

Watch *Mildred Pierce* with *Mommie Dearest*. It's fun in a perverse way to watch *Mildred Pierce*, knowing that Joan, unlike her character, who did everything *for* her kids, in real life actually did everything *to* them. She really did deserve that Academy Award! The director hated Joan, addressed her as "Phony Joannie," and once demanded that she remove her shoulder pads. "But," said Crawford tearfully, "I'm not wearing any."

AFTERMATH

Although this movie revitalized Joan's flagging career, it did little to stop her continued descent into child abuse, alcoholism, and fright wigs.

Stepmom (1998)
Rated PG-13

Directed by Chris Columbus
Starring Julia Roberts, Susan Sarandon, Ed Harris, Jena Malone, Liam Aiken

THE PLOT

Successful photographer Isabelle Kelly (Julia Roberts) has just moved in with boyfriend Luke Harrison (Ed Harris), a prominent lawyer who has two children with his ex-wife, Jackie (Susan Sarandon). The younger kid, Ben (Liam Aiken), is somewhat accepting of Isabelle, while the 12-year-old Anna (Jena Malone) is downright hostile, an attitude encouraged by her mother. Isabelle keeps trying to connect with the kids, sometimes jeopardizing her career, but no matter how hard she tries, she keeps battling with Jackie and getting guff from Anna. Right around the same time that Luke and Isabelle decide to get married, Jackie has a recurrence of cancer and the extended family is thrown into crisis.

Considering that half of all Americans now live in a stepfamily, it's odd that there aren't more movies about this complicated dynamic. (And no, *Snow White* doesn't count.) Let's hope that most stepdaughters are not as nasty to their stepmoms as Anna is to Isabelle, saying

MATCH THE TATTOO WITH ITS OWNER

1. Yellow pear on left buttock   *a. Drew Barrymore*

2. Crucifix on left ankle   *b. Kennedy*

3. Woodstock from *Peanuts* on left breast   *c. Carré Otis*

4. Japanese chrysanthemum on right buttock   *d. Janeane Garofalo*

5. Flowers on lower stomach   *e. Courtney Love*

6. Bracelet on left wrist   *f. Melanie Griffith*

7. Pink elephant on groin   *g. Julia Roberts*

8. Ankle bracelet on ankle   *h. Traci Lords*

9. Chinese character for strength on shoulder   *i. Cher*

10. *Think* on right arm   *j. Whoopi Goldberg*

Answers: 1.(f) 2.(h) 3.(j) 4.(i) 5.(a) 6.(c) 7.(b) 8.(e) 9.(g) 10.(d)

things like "*You're* my problem," "I'm allergic to you," and that stock taunt of stepkids everywhere, "You're not my mother!" Stepfamilies are hard for everybody, and while the vast majority of stepfamilies are not as moneyed or good-looking as the *Stepmom* gang, it's encouraging that there is a mainstream Hollywood movie that explores this charged territory.

Bonding Potential: 6

Isabelle, winsome though she is, just can't seem to win over her stepkids. She gets them tickets to a Pearl Jam concert and takes the kids to glamorous photo shoots. She even buys them an adorable puppy, though we just know she's the one who'll get stuck walking it at one in the morning. Nothing works.

Of course, Jackie the supermom is a big part of the problem. When Ben asks his mother, "Do you think Isabelle's pretty?" Mom's reply is "Sure . . . if you like big teeth." Hey, we're talking about Julia Roberts here, not Heather Mills McCartney. Here are two strong women facing off with the family as a battlefield. Jackie is jealous of Isabelle, Isabelle is jealous of Jackie, Anna is jealous of everybody, and Dad is stuck in the middle. In short, it's business as usual in a stepfamily. It takes a tragedy to bring this family together, creating what is nowadays euphemistically known as the blended family.

35

 Hunk Factor: 5

Ed Harris is a hunk. Not a scream-out-loud hunk, but still adorable in that stalwart way.

 Hankie Factor: 7

It has cancer, after all.

Squirming in Your Seat Watching a Sex Scene with Your Mother/Daughter Factor: 0

BEHIND THE SCENES

When Ben is in the hospital, Isabelle sings him the song "If I Needed You." Julia Roberts's former husband, Lyle Lovett, recorded this tune for his 1998 album *Step Inside This House.*

AFTERMATH

In 2001, a Louisiana teenager named Shaun Muffet, in a snit with his stepmom, stabbed her to death with a carving knife. We have no idea whether he saw *Stepmom* or not.

OLDER TEENS ONLY

Cruel Intentions (1999)

Rated R

36

Directed by Roger Kumble

Starring Sarah Michelle Gellar, Ryan Philippe, Reese Witherspoon, Selma Blair, Sean Patrick Leonard

THE PLOT

In this update of the juicy 1782 novel *Les Liaisons Dangereuses,* Sarah Michelle Gellar and Ryan Philippe star as Kathryn and Sebastian, depraved stepsiblings who live together in an elegant New York townhouse. There's no sign of parental supervision, but they are bankrolled by weekly allowances that could probably float small Latin American countries. Devious and maniacal don't even begin to describe these two kids. They have the usual teenage hobbies: manipulating their prep school classmates, snorting coke, indulging their semi-incestuous longing for each other, and when all else fails, seducing and then destroying innocent freshmen like Cecile (Selma Blair). Kathryn makes Sebastian, a twelfth grade Don Juan, a bet he cannot refuse: Deflower the headmaster's beautiful daughter Annette (Reese Witherspoon). If he fails, she gets his convertible; if he wins, he gets to bed Kathryn.

Teens in the throes of zits and SATs won't be able to resist the decadent fantasy world of Kathryn and Sebastian; they wear designer clothes, drive classic sport cars, and best of all, never have any homework. Perhaps more importantly, *Cruel Intentions* will provide an introduction to Stephen Frears's far superior movie, *Dangerous Liaisons*.

 ### Bonding Potential: 5

Few of the kids and none of the adults are any match for Kathryn and Sebastian's Machiavellian maneuvers. Mothers may as well find out, and sooner rather than later, that their offspring are unable to resist a movie where adults are reduced to buffoons. Kathryn shows Cecile's mother (Christine Baranski) the crucifix around her neck as evidence of her religious devotion. Yet as soon as the clueless mother leaves, what does that rotten girl do but open up her cross—a cocaine vial (!)—to indulge in a little bit of salvation not taught in Sunday school. But, moms, don't despair: The ending of *Cruel Intentions* shows what filmmakers call the "redemptive power of love."

37

Hunk Factor: 7

Note to Ryan Philippe: Stop posing, please! You look great in clothes, but this is a movie, not a *GQ* cover! Moms, be aware that Ryan's character is, to put it politely, an antihero: a heart-to-heart discussion of hunkiness versus skunkiness is definitely in order. Sean Patrick Leonard is too earnest to be sexy: Wait for him in *Save the Last Dance*.

Hankie Factor: 2

You may need them for the ending.

Squirming in Your Seat Watching a Sex Scene with Your
Mother/Daughter Factor: 9

There's plenty of sex, though none of it is terribly graphic. The squirmiest moments are provided by the film's dialogue, including when Kathryn promises Sebastian that if he wins the bet, he can "put it anywhere."

BEHIND THE SCENES

The year 1999 was a busy one for Reese and Ryan. First, this movie was released, then they married in June, and in August they had their first baby, Ava.

AFTERMATH

Blair and Geller won the MTV Movie Award for best kiss.

The Opposite of Sex (1998)
Rated R

Directed by Don Roos
Starring Christina Ricci, Martin Donovan, Lisa Kudrow, Ivan Sergei, Lyle Lovett

THE PLOT

Let's not mince words: DeeDee Truit (Christina Ricci) is a slutty sociopath. What's more, at the tender age of sixteen, she's completely jaded. After her despised stepfather dies, she leaves her equally despised mother and heads to Indiana to move in with her gay half brother, Bill (Martin Donovan). She proceeds to seduce Bill's beautiful but dumb partner Matt (Ivan Sergei) and claims to be pregnant by him. This infuriates Bill's friend, the *very* priggish Lucia (Lisa Kudrow), who has been suspicious and resentful of DeeDee from the beginning. The whole affair erupts into a scandal when one of Bill's former students falsely accuses him of sexual abuse. The local sheriff (Lyle Lovett) gets involved, motivated more by his crush on Lucia than anything else.

From the beginning, DeeDee lets us know that she's *really* nasty: "If you think I'm just plucky, then you're out of luck. I *don't* have a heart of gold and I *don't* grow one later, okay?" So why do we keep rooting for her after she does so many terrible things? Maybe it's her straight-talking, deadpan narration. At one point she addresses the females in the audience, warning them if their dates were squeamish during the scene where men were kissing, then they're probably gay.

 Bonding Potential: 6

DeeDee really hates her mother, and from the opening scenes, it's evident that the feeling is mutual. Still, we maintain that *The Opposite of Sex* earns its bonding factor of 6. All women—mothers and daughters included—should hear the story of a bad girl who shakes up the lives of everybody she meets. This is the kind of role that *always* goes to the guys. Why should they be the only ones allowed to be offensive and in-your-face? DeeDee is a heroine (using the term loosely) who shocks people from the opening to the closing credits. An example is when she dismisses her stepfather's death from colon cancer: "It couldn't have been a more appropriate way for that asshole to go."

An aside: Lucia has a poignant moment when she speaks about her mother's reaction to finding out her son is gay. "She said, 'It's such a lonely life.' She said that to a single, straight girl . . . isn't that funny?"

Hunk Factor: 6

Martin Donovan and Sergei are cute. Lyle Lovett looks like—well, Lyle Lovett.

39

Hankie Factor: 0

 Squirming in Your Seat Watching a Sex Scene with Your Mother/Daughter Factor: 6

DeeDee is promiscuous, after all. So there are some scenes that are inappropriate for younger girls.

HOTTIES FOR DAUGHTERS

1. Vin Diesel, *The Fast and the Furious*

2. Heath Ledger, *The Patriot*

3. Jet Li, *Romeo Must Die*

4. Josh Hartnett, *Black Hawk Down*

5. Leonardo DiCaprio, *Gangs of New York*

6. Tyrese, *2 Fast, 2 Furious*

7. Ashton Kutcher, *Just Married*

8. Trent Ford, *How to Deal*

9. Ryan Philippe, *Gosford Park*

10. Orlando Bloom, *Pirates of the Caribbean*

BEHIND THE SCENES

Lisa Kudrow, internationally known as Phoebe on *Friends*, commented that her character Lucia would hate her character Phoebe.

AFTERMATH

Some gays protested that DeeDee's voice-over was borderline offensive.

Traffic (2000)
Rated R

Directed by Steven Soderbergh
Starring Michael Douglas, Catherine Zeta-Jones, Benicio Del Toro, Amy Irving, Erika
Christensen, Don Cheadle

41

THE PLOT

Traffic uses four separate plotlines to depict our country's losing war on drugs and drug trafficking. Robert Wakefield (Michael Douglas), America's new drug czar, sets out to combat illegal drugs in the United States, in Mexico, and as it turns out, in his own family. His world is turned upside down when he and his wife Barbara (Amy Irving) discover that their daughter Caroline (Erika Christensen) is a drug addict. The other plots concern a Mexican cop (Benicio Del Toro), a San Diego DEA agent (Don Cheadle), and a millionaire dealer's pampered wife (Catherine Zeta-Jones).

This dope opera has everything—great script, direction, and acting—but more important, it tackles teenage drug abuse with intelligence and sensitivity. Caroline Wakefield is every mother's worst nightmare. There is no antidrug speech a mom can make that would have more of an impact than watching Caroline's descent from honor student to crack whore.

Bonding Potential: 7

Let's be honest: All mothers, in varying degrees, sanitize part of their past, whether it be smoking pot, throwing up into their purse, or dating guys who had perms. *Traffic* touches on this when Mom, discussing Caroline's drug abuse, admits to her husband, "We've all had our moments. Lord knows I've tried every drug there was." That's okay with him; he sees her behavior as different from her daughter's. "You *experimented*!" he cries. Some mothers might feel uncomfortable watching Barbara agonizing over her daughter's drug abuse while guzzling scotch. Both parents self-medicate with alcohol, rationalizing that they need to drink since it "takes the edge off." They're as much in denial as their daughter.

 Hunk Factor: 7

We find Benicio Del Toro, oversized head notwithstanding, a worthy sex symbol. But the big hunk payoff doesn't come until Benjamin Bratt makes his all-too-brief appearance. Michael Douglas may have evolved into a really good actor, but he hasn't been cute since *The Streets of San Francisco* was on television.

 Hankie Factor: 2

The expression on Benicio Del Toro's face in the last scene might call for a hankie or two.

Squirming in Your Seat Watching a Sex Scene with Your Mother/Daughter Factor: 4

Caroline is in bed with a crack dealer, a scene with no erotic content but still very uncomfortable to watch.

BEHIND THE SCENES

Michael Douglas dealt with his son Cameron's real-life struggle with drugs, making especially poignant his speech from *Traffic:* "If there is a war on drugs, then many of our family members are the enemy. And I don't know how you wage war on your own family." Screenwriter Stephen Gaghan drew on his own personal experience—he, like Caroline, was an honor student *and* a drug addict in high school.

AFTERMATH

In *Traffic*, Catherine Zeta-Jones played pregnant and was pregnant. After the movie, she gave birth to son Dylan and later married Dylan's dad, Michael Douglas. *Traffic* won four Oscars, including, we're happy to say, Best Supporting Actor for Benicio Del Toro.

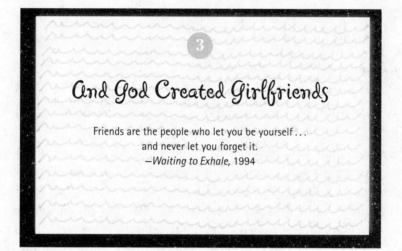

And God Created Girlfriends

Friends are the people who let you be yourself...
and never let you forget it.
—*Waiting to Exhale*, 1994

Boyfriends—and (gasp) sometimes even husbands—come and go. Your dog may abandon you for a chew toy. And yes, someday even your mother will die and go to heaven. But girlfriends are forever. You can tell them your deepest secrets, biggest fears, and wildest dreams, and you know they won't laugh. Best of all, they don't care if you're not wearing any makeup, have bad breath, or for that matter, have put bathing on the back burner for a while. They give you the freedom to be who you are while stopping you from going overboard. Girlfriends are one of life's true gifts.

A League of Their Own (1992)

Rated PG

Directed by Penny Marshall

Starring Tom Hanks, Geena Davis, Madonna, Lori Petty, Rosie O'Donnell, Jon Lovitz, Garry Marshall

THE PLOT

World War II begins and the nation's men, including its baseball players, go off to fight. Baseball club owner Walter Harvey (Garry Marshall) attempts to save the sport by founding the All American Girls Professional Baseball League. The league gets off to a rocky start, but the girls ham it up, play good ball, and slowly develop a following. The movie follows the story of the Rockford Peaches, focusing on their star pitcher, Dottie Hinson (Geena Davis), and the manager, a baseball great turned lush, Jimmy Dugan (Tom Hanks). Also playing for the Peaches are Mae (Madonna), Doris (Rosie O'Donnell), and Kit Keller (Lori Petty), who's Dottie's whiny kid sister.

It took Penny Marshall, Hollywood's most successful woman director, to bring this little-known chapter in baseball (and women's) history to the screen. The league played until 1954, yet it wasn't until 1988 that they were honored by the Baseball Hall of Fame.

Bonding Potential: 7

Today even the youngest girls participate in all kind of sporting events and competitions. Yet there was a time in the not-so-distant past when women were forced to sublimate their athletic abilities and interests. Even Dottie, a player so gifted that Dugan tells her "baseball is what lights you up," refuses to take the game seriously. She is, after all, a wife.

Also, women athletes used to be considered "funny," a code word for lesbian. As Doris, Rosie O'Donnell addresses this: "The other boys

46

made me feel like I was wrong. Like I was a weird girl or a strange girl, or not even a girl just 'cause I could play ball." Another player remarks of Doris, "She reminds me of my husband."

 **Hunk Factor: 1**

Tom Hanks is somewhat endearing despite the fact that he's slobbering tobacco juice.

 Hankie Factor: 3

In the locker room and in front of all of her teammates, Betty Spaghetti (Tracy Reiner) receives a telegram stating that her husband was killed. Just when we had forgotten there was a war going on!

Squirming in Your Seat Watching a Sex Scene with Your Mother/Daughter Factor: 0

BEHIND THE SCENES

Penny Marshall introduced Madonna and Rosie O'Donnell to each other, saying, "You're going to play best friends, so you better be friends." They did become friends, and some years later, Madonna hosted the baby shower for Rosie's first child, Parker.

AFTERMATH

A TV series based on the movie struck out, but director Penny Marshall and Rosie O'Donnell did a bunch of Kmart commercials together.

Beaches (1988)

Rated PG-13

Directed by Garry Marshall

Starring Bette Midler, Barbara Hershey, John Heard, Spalding Gray, Lainie Kazan

THE PLOT

Beaches chronicles the lives of street-smart CC (Bette Midler) and book-smart Hillary (Barbara Hershey), who meet in Atlantic City as young girls and become pen pals, then best friends. CC grows up to become, well, the Divine Miss M, and Hillary, a lawyer and single mother, finds herself constantly torn between her ideals and her upbringing. Their unlikely friendship survives decades, crappy New York apartments, ridiculous hairstyles, tumultuous careers, troubled marriages, much heartache, but alas, not congenital heart failure.

48

Every video store should have a special section, curtained off, poorly lit, where they stash away all the films you're not only embarrassed to acknowledge you rent, but ashamed to admit you actually love. *Beaches* would be right there between *Untamed Heart* and *Anne of Avonlea*. It's a guilty pleasure on par with Krispy Kreme donuts. *Beaches* makes for a cathartic double bill with *Terms of Endearment*. In fact, this movie is basically *Terms of Endearment* with musical numbers. Be sure to have a full box of Kleenex handy.

Bonding Potential: 8

Sure, *Beaches* is a cheesy, formulaic tearjerker, but its view of female friendship is both realistic and generous, and the women bring out the best and worst in one another. And in the film's second half, you can appreciate not only the warm and tender relationship between ailing Hillary and her young daughter, but the bond that forms, first hesitantly and then with great gusto, between the girl and CC.

When you're not holding back tears, you're choking back laughter.

Between the corny flashbacks, the cornier soundtrack, and the screamingly bad wardrobe choices, *Beaches* is rife with opportunities for wisecrackers, young and old.

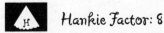 Hunk Factor: 5

John Heard, best known as the father from *Home Alone,* is surprisingly cute as the experimental theater director who romances both Hillary and CC.

Hankie Factor: 8

Beaches tugs at the heartstrings with a heavy hand, but Midler marches straight through the middle of this melodrama like a big brass band. Still, as CC crescendos, Hillary fades, and you'd best wear your waterproof mascara.

49

Squirming in Your Seat Watching a Sex Scene with Your Mother/Daughter Factor: 0

You're more likely to squirm at Midler's untamed frizz.

BEHIND THE SCENES

Barbara Hershey prepared for the role of young Hillary with Robert De Niro–like weight gain—by getting collagen injections in her lips.

AFTERMATH

Midler earned a Grammy for the song "Wind Beneath My Wings," which plays over what must have been the film's forty-seventh musical montage. It also went on to become the most-requested song ever at weddings, proms, and funerals.

The Color Purple (1985)
Rated PG-13

Directed by Steven Spielberg

Starring Danny Glover, Whoopi Goldberg, Margaret Avery, Oprah Winfrey, Lawrence
Fishburne, Willard Pugh, Akosua Busia, Desreta Jackson, Adolph Caesar,
Leonard Jackson

THE PLOT

Based on Alice Walker's novel, this is the poignant, hopeful story of
Celie (Whoopi Goldberg), a black woman in the South at the early part
of the twentieth century, whom we follow from childhood into middle
age. She is subjugated to and the control of her transferred from an
abusive father (Desreta Jackson) to an abusive husband (Danny
Glover). Not only do they co-opt her power, but they separate her
from the joy and the love in her life. Her father takes Celie's children
away from her at birth, and her husband, whom she calls Mister,
sends away her sister, Nettie (Akosua Busia), "the only person in the
world who loves her." These men continue a legacy of things not
sorted out—cyclical abuse, both emotional and psychological, that is
passed from generation to generation. Along the way, Celie meets a
series of other women who shape her life. She befriends bossy boots
Sofia (Oprah Winfrey), wife of Mister's son Harpo (Willard Pugh), who
is nobody's fool. And when Mister's beautiful, heavy-drinking, juke-
joint-singing mistress Shug (Margaret Avery) comes to stay with
them, Celie is relieved—Mister doesn't beat her when Shug is around.
Eventually she and Shug develop a fondness for each other, perhaps
more than a fondness (although their physical relationship is not
drawn as clearly here as in the book), and Celie is transformed by being noticed.

The lives of black women in this time and place are arduous, but
these women live through and triumph over poverty, abuse, prejudice, and powerlessness. *The Color Purple* is about relationships,
love, understanding, growth, and redemption, as these women travel

from darkness into the light. When Shug tells Celie she has a beautiful smile, Celie believes her. Shug brings Celie to the first step of claiming her power.

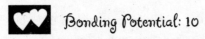 Bonding Potential: 10

The Color Purple is about women growing beyond the extraordinary and concrete limitations in their lives. In short, it's about overcoming victimization. At one point Mister says to Celie, "You're black, you're poor, you're ugly, you're a woman. You're nothing at all!" She shows him and us, too. This story is about triumph and forgiveness—even the most brutal oppressor shows hope for redemption.

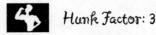 Hunk Factor: 3

Three words: Young Lawrence Fishburne.

51

 Hankie Factor: 10

Hankies *required*.

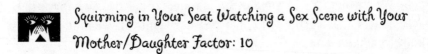 Squirming in Your Seat Watching a Sex Scene with Your Mother/Daughter Factor: 10

The sex scenes, not to be confused with love scenes, are not explicitly depicted, but they are emotionally tough.

BEHIND THE SCENES

After Whoopi Goldberg read *The Color Purple*, "I sat down and wrote to Alice Walker . . . telling her that I would go anywhere to audition if this was made into a movie. Walker's letter of response: Dear Whoopi:

I know who you are, I've been to your shows, and I've already suggested you for the role."

AFTERMATH

Oprah Winfrey, who didn't own a pair of shoes until she was 5, became the first African-American on *Forbes* magazine's billionaire list.

Mystic Pizza (1988)
Rated R

Directed by Donald Petrie
Starring Annabeth Gish, Julia Roberts, Lili Taylor, Vincent D'Onofrio, Adam Storke

THE PLOT

It's hard to get out of working-class Mystic, Connecticut, as the three main characters, Kat Arujo (Annabeth Gish), Daisy Arujo (Julia Roberts), and Jojo Barboza (Lili Taylor), are finding out. All three descend from Portuguese fishermen, work at the Mystic Pizza Parlor, and are looking for a way out of town. The movie opens with Jojo fainting at the altar because marrying the man she loves (Vincent D'Onofrio) means spending the rest of her life in Mystic. Kat, working her way through Yale, falls for the married father of her babysitting charge while Daisy, the wild one, sets her sights on wealthy Charles Gordon Windsor Jr. (Adam Storke).

Mystic Pizza follows the interwoven lives of these three young women as they grapple with love, friendship, and belonging. And that's just for openers. As their stories unfold, we get a lot of big eighties hair, purposely ripped T-shirts, and Julia Roberts in a short black dress with an enormous white bow on the chest.

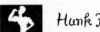 Bonding Potential: 6

Mystic Pizza, in large part, is about how young women relate to and support one another. After JoJo bails out of her wedding, there is no one to whom she can make the following confession *except* her girlfriends: "I saw myself ten years from now, fat and ugly, picking up all these kids swarming around me and picking fish scales out of Bill's boot."

There's also a scene that will make for an interesting discussion about class. Daisy stands in front of her refrigerator and is disdainful of the ubiquitous lobsters therein, since it represents her mother's dead-end life of preparing lobsters to be sold. Later, when she goes to her rich boyfriend's house for dinner, she sees how some people perceive lobster as a delicacy.

 Hunk Factor: 1

Slim pickings.

 Hankie Factor: 2

There are a few touching, albeit dry, moments.

Squirming in Your Seat Watching a Sex Scene with Your Mother/Daughter Factor: 2

Sexual scenes in the movie might provide a squirm factor for younger or more reserved viewers.

BEHIND THE SCENES

Look for Matt Damon in his first movie role, playing Charlie's younger brother.

AFTERMATH

This was Julia Roberts's fourth movie and the one that made her a name. She earned $50,000 for *Mystic Pizza* and went on to be the highest earning actress to date, demanding $20 million per picture. We suspect Matt Damon, likewise, had an exponential wage increase.

The Truth About Cats and Dogs (1996)
Rated PG-13

Directed by Michael Lehmann
Starring Janeane Garofalo, Uma Thurman, Ben Chaplin, Jamie Foxx

THE PLOT

54

In theory it just shouldn't work: a latter-day Cyrano de Bergerac as a call-in radio host for pets and their beleaguered owners? Who instead of composing lyric verse talks depressed goldfish back up out of the toilet bowl? It shouldn't work, but it does, wonderfully, thanks in no small part to its Cyrano—Abby (Janeane Garofalo). In *The Truth About Cats and Dogs,* Garofalo, best known for her smart, acerbic stand-up, plays the radio veterinarian who's good with animals, less so with men. When Brian (Ben Chaplin), a British photographer, calls up, desperate for advice about a humongous panicky roller-skating dog, Abby wins him over with her confident voice and charming wit. Enamored and intrigued, he asks to meet her in person.

Of course had Abby and Brian met for coffee, fallen in love, and opened their own pet modeling agency, well, that wouldn't be much of a movie. Thus Abby, insecure that she can't live up to the promise of her voice, conscripts her neighbor—tall beautiful blonde Noelle (Uma Thurman)—to meet Brian in her stead. What ensues, of course, is a funny, sweet series of mistaken identity mix-ups and love triangulations, as Brian romances Noelle in person (believing her to be a certain radio vet) and spends hours on the phone with Abby discussing everything from fine literature to sandwich making.

The plot requires us to believe that Abby, though possessing of a perfectly normal-sized nose, is as ugly as an Elephant Woman standing next to Noelle; that she's the kind of girl described by matchmak-

GALS WITH GAY GUYS AS BEST FRIENDS

1. Parminder K. Nagra (best friend Ameet Chana), *Bend It Like Beckham*

2. Winona Ryder (best friend Steve Zahn), *Reality Bites*

3. Gene Tierney (best friend Clifton Webb), *Laura*

4. Julia Roberts (best friend Rupert Everett), *My Best Friend's Wedding*

5. Jennifer Aniston (best friend Paul Rudd), *The Object of My Affection*

6. Madonna (best friend Rupert Everett), *The Next Best Thing*

7. Doris Day (best friend Tony Randall), *Pillow Talk*

8. Helen Hunt (best friend Greg Kinnear), *As Good as It Gets*

9. Anne Baxter (best friend George Sanders), *All About Eve*

10. Nastassja Kinski (best friend Robert Downey Jr.), *One Night Stand*

11. Natalie Wood (best friend Sal Mineo), *Rebel Without a Cause*

12. Liza Minnelli (best friend Michael York), *Cabaret*

ers as having a "good personality"—that she might in fact be at her most attractive as a dissociated voice. This is, of course, rubbish, and we see immediately what Brian takes two hours of movie to discover: Janeane Garofalo is beautiful.

 Bonding Potential: 8

The Truth About Cats and Dogs has more to offer than mere farcical charades; it addresses, albeit with a light hand, the very real problem of low self-esteem among women. Years of being overlooked by men have left Abby insecure and defensive, and who could blame her? And Noelle, the willowy, near anorexic model, is also plagued by self-doubt: Being objectified for a living and emotionally abused by her no-good boyfriend/manager has left her timid and trepidatious. The two women forge an easy and supportive friendship, which the movie addresses at least as much as it does either woman's romance with Brian. In most Cyrano adaptations, the good-looking mouthpiece through which Cyrano woos his lady love is not much more than a buffoonish, albeit attractive, ventriloquist's dummy. Here, the film is as generous with Noelle as it is with Abby; she is ditzy, sure, but eager to learn, curious when another film might have made her arrogant. The relationship that grows between these two women is complex and believable.

 Hunk Factor: 7

It's no surprise that British charmer Ben Chaplin wins over both Abby and Noelle; his soulful eyes and adorable accent are irresistible. Also hunkworthy is comedian Jamie Foxx, who plays Brian's best friend.

Hankie Factor: 0

Squirming in Your Seat Watching a Sex Scene with Your Mother/Daughter Factor: 6

There's not much in the way of nudity or graphic sexual content, but Abby and Brian engage in some phone sex that's a little uncomfortable to watch, whether or not you're viewing it with family.

BEHIND THE SCENES

Not even our trusty heroine is immune to the pressures of Hollywood: The last scene, reshot a few months after the rest of the film had been completed, boasts a noticeably thinner Janeane Garofalo.

In order to fit into certain shots with the six-foot Thurman, Garofalo, five-one, had to stand on a wooden box.

AFTERMATH

Garofalo has since struggled to find a role so perfectly suited to her. Thurman recently starred in *Kill Bill,* which director Quentin Tarantino wrote especially for her.

Romy and Michele's High School Reunion (1997)
Rated R

Directed by David Mirkin

Starring Mira Sorvino, Lisa Kudrow, Janeane Garofalo, Alan Cumming, Julia Campbell, Camryn Manheim, Vincent Ventresca

THE PLOT

Romy (Mira Sorvino) and Michele (Lisa Kudrow), best friends since high school (they had their senior picture taken together), made a break from Tucson for the bright lights of L.A. Taking ditziness to a new level, they go about their lives as roommates who make their own clothes, go clubbing, and have watched *Pretty Woman* together over twenty times ("I just love it when they let her shop!"). One day Heather Mooney (Janeane Garofalo) wanders up to Romy, a cashier at the Jaguar dealership, and lets her know that their high school reunion is coming up. Remembering the agony of being outcasts, Romy and Michele deliberate about going to the reunion since they don't have boyfriends and Michele is unemployed (Romy wears her underemployment proudly).

Everything changes when they hatch a plan to make up a story about how fabulous their lives are. This is where the fun really starts, in a tarted-up *Dumb and Dumber* sort of way. They get their hands on a Jaguar convertible, dress themselves in dark "businesswomen" suits (with hairdos to match), and set out to tell their former schoolmates that they are wealthy entrepreneurs, the inventors of Post-it notes. Trying to determine who is responsible for which aspects of the invention process gives us one of the best jokes in the movie: They argue over who is the Mary and who is the Rhoda. They reminisce (via flashbacks) about their school days as they look through their yearbook and give us the 411 on the gang: Sandy Frink (Alan Cumming), the übernerd who longed for Michele; Heather Mooney, the black-clad self-proclaimed loser who longed for Sandy Frink; Billy Christiansen (Vincent Ventresca), the "hottest guy in school," on whom Romy still has a crush; Toby Walters (Camryn Manheim), the pimply, braces-wearing class do-gooder who just wants to be everyone's friend; and the ubiquitous A group, who tortured everyone else. When the girls head to the desert, fun and laughs ensue and everyone gets their due.

Janeane Garofalo always picks up the pace, but Alan Cumming steals every scene he's in. The eighties music is surpassed only by Mona May's costumes (she also did costumes for *Clueless* and *The Wedding Singer*).

Bonding Potential: 6

Beneath all of the fun and fluff are some good lessons, and from beginning to end this movie is about girlfriends.

Hunk Factor: 3

Billy, played by Vincent Ventresca, is attractive in that cutest-guy-in-high-school-who-becomes-a-loser kind of way.

 Hankie Factor: 0

Cheers, no tears.

Squirming in Your Seat Watching a Sex Scene with Your Mother/Daughter Factor: 1

There is a feigned sex scene with audio only and played for laughs—to the lads on the other side of the door.

BEHIND THE SCENES

Lisa Kudrow made up the entire "special glue" riff on the spot.

AFTERMATH

Lisa Kudrow, Mira Sorvino, and Alan Cumming were nominated for an MTV Award: best dance sequence. A television show called *Romy and Michele: In the Beginning,* written by Robin Schiff, is in the works.

OLDER TEENS ONLY

Muriel's Wedding (1994)

Rated R

Directed by P. J. Hogan

Starring Toni Collette, Bill Hunter, Rachel Griffiths, Jeanie Drynan, Gennie Nevinson

THE PLOT

Muriel Heslop (Toni Collette) spends her time in Porpoise Spit, Australia, listening to ABBA music. ABBA is one of the many things about her life that stink: She's an unattractive, overweight, secretary-school dropout who is stuck with a dysfunctional family and a set of bitchy girlfriends. Also, we suspect she's a mouth breather. Even though she's never had a date, she spends most of her time dreaming about her wedding day, pasting up pictures of brides and studying every frame of Princess Di's wedding video. After she hooks up with her first truly supportive friend, the wild and crazy Rhonda (Rachel Griffiths), she moves to Sydney, changes her name to "Mariel," and begins a new life.

Muriel's Wedding begs the immortal question: Can a girl whose nervous tick involves erratic tongue movements find true happiness? It also offers this valuable fashion lesson: Studded black leather pants are not for everyone.

♥♥ *Bonding Potential:* 8

It's hard to think of a movie character with less going for her than Muriel. Even nervous Charlotte Vale of *Now, Voyager* lived in a mansion, unlike Muriel, who lives in plastic-coated digs with a television-addicted family. Muriel's father, Bill (Bill Hunter), is a philandering gasbag who hates the sight of his wife and kids.

Muriel's Wedding shows how one parent's verbal abuse can kill a family's spirit. The Heslop kids are couch potatoes and their mother Betty (Jeanie Drynan) has been reduced to a vegetative state. Betty is sympathetic but so defeated that we see how her weakness is even more deadly than Bill's cruelty. Daughters who feel that their mothers are too intrusive will see a mom who has given up on mothering and on life, and may appreciate their mother's involvement.

To survive, Muriel must leave her family, and it's Rhonda who makes this happen. The most touching scene in the movie is Muriel's tribute to Rhonda: "When I lived in Porpoise Spit, I used to sit in my room for hours and listen to ABBA songs. But since I've met you and moved to Sydney, I haven't listened to one ABBA song. That's because my life is as good as an ABBA song. It's as good as 'Dancing Queen.'"

Hunk Factor: 0

Hankie Factor: 4

Muriel's mother is heartbreaking.

Squirming in Your Seat Watching a Sex Scene with Your Mother/Daughter Factor: 7

You'll squirm, but you'll laugh. Rachel Griffiths got in some practice for her future role as Brenda in HBO's *Six Feet Under*. Like Brenda, Rhonda is a sex addict who indulges in the occasional threesome.

AFTERMATH

The movie won three Australian Academy Awards: best picture; best actress (Collette); best supporting actress (Griffiths).

61

Thelma and Louise (1991)

Rated R

Directed by Ridley Scott

Starring Susan Sarandon, Geena Davis, Harvey Keitel, Michael Madsen, Brad Pitt

THE PLOT

Girlfriends Louise (Susan Sarandon) and Thelma (Geena Davis) take off for a fishing trip in a 1966 Thunderbird convertible, leaving behind their stultifying lives in small-town Arkansas and, respectively, an indifferent boyfriend and a boorish husband. The first night out, Louise saves Thelma from a rapist, telling him, "In the future, when a woman is crying like that, she isn't having any fun." When the creep goads them on, Louise shoots him and the two women become outlaws. A kindhearted detective (Harvey Keitel) follows their trail throughout the Southwest.

This is the greatest chick road picture of all. *Thelma and Louise* is funny, sad, powerful, and as *Rolling Stone* puts it, "begins like an episode of *I Love Lucy* and ends with the impact of *Easy Rider*."

Bonding Potential: 8

Thelma and Louise celebrates the strength of female friendship. Neither woman has any family to speak of, so Louise serves as a mother figure to the younger, naive Thelma. Around Louise, Thelma comes into her own: she blows up an eighteen-wheeler and at one point critiques her overbearing husband's body: "You could park a car in the shadow of Daryl's ass." Talk about empowerment! The characters are liberated because of the strength they draw from their relationship, an affirming message for girlfriends of all ages.

Hunk Factor: 7

Thelma and Louise introduced the world to Brad Pitt. Michael Madsen, as Louise's boyfriend, is sexy and soulful. And we're happy to report that, as a welcome change of pace, Harvey Keitel keeps his clothes on.

 Hankie Factor: 4

You won't need hankies till the end credits roll.

 Squirming in Your Seat Watching a Sex Scene with Your Mother/Daughter Factor: 5

A modicum of squirming might occur during the Brad/Geena love scene (no body doubles, by the way).

BEHIND THE SCENES

Even though she was too tall for him, Geena Davis and Brad Pitt had an affair during filming. This no doubt contributed to the realism of the above scene.

AFTERMATH

Before its release, studio execs were wary of the film, afraid the public would not be interested in a story about "two bitches in a car." They quickly changed their minds after the movie opened to enthusiastic reviews.

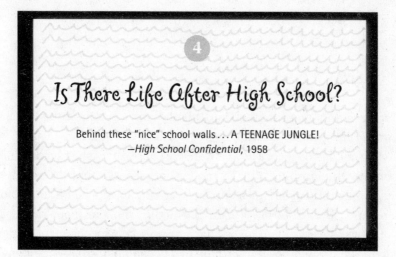

Is There Life After High School?

Behind these "nice" school walls . . . A TEENAGE JUNGLE!
—*High School Confidential*, 1958

(*Note*: If you were or still are popular in high school, just skip the following paragraph and go straight to the movies.)

When you're in that seventh circle of hell that grown-ups insist on calling high school, try to remember that the smug, zit-free, know-it-all popular kids are at their peak. Their lives will never get any better than this. High school misfits are the future success stories, so remember, the tables will turn—you'll see.

Bring It On (2000)

Rated PG-13

Directed by Peyton Reed

Starring Kirsten Dunst, Eliza Dushku, Jesse Bradford, Gabrielle Union, Clare Kramer, Nicole Bilderback, Tsianina Joelson, Nathan West, Huntley Ritter

THE PLOT

Torrance Shipman (Kirsten Dunst) is the new captain of the Rancho Carne High School cheerleading squad in suburban San Diego. The Toros squad is no joke: They've won five consecutive cheerleading national championships. But Torrance soon realizes that the routines that brought them so much success were in fact ripped off, move for move (by former Toros captain Big Red), from the inner-city East Compton Clovers. The Clovers have always known about the stolen routines but could never afford the trip to championships—until now.

With tough girl newcomer Missy (Eliza Dushku) by her side, and the championships only three weeks away, Torrance struggles to come up with a whole new routine. Meanwhile, Isis (Gabrielle Union), captain of the Clovers, is determined to bring her team to victory, and the movie climaxes with the squads going head to head at the national championships in Daytona Beach, Florida.

The ugliness of high school is peppered with good friends, cute boys, and youthful passion. *Bring It On* manages to be funny without being mean or cynical. It's a fun and amusing romp with a lot of teen navels. What more do you want?

Bonding Potential: 6

Bring It On is not exactly a serious treatise on race relations. Still, it's not every day that a frothy, frivolous cheerleading comedy gives some thought to the injustice of whites appropriating (ahem, totally stealing) black music and culture. And the movie brandishes a few satirically sharp edges at the snobbery of the affluent Toros. "That's all right, that's okay. You're gonna pump our gas someday," the Rancho Grande squad chants to rivals from a less well-heeled school district.

 Hunk Factor: 3

There are some hunky Ken doll male cheerleaders along with the positively adorable Cliff (Jesse Bradford).

 Hankie Factor: 0

 Squirming in Your Seat Watching a Sex Scene with Your Mother/Daughter Factor: 0

BEHIND THE SCENES

It was originally called "Cheer Fever" and was influenced by the 1930s director/choreographer Busby Berkeley. Director Peyton Reed had a unique take on cheerleaders: "If you took cheerleaders to another country or another planet and showed them—it is very obvious that it is a rite of passage with a very sexual aspect to it. There's an innocent quality to it, but also a sexuality." (Huh?)

AFTERMATH

Kirsten Dunst started her own production company, Wooden Spoon, a tribute to women's crafts and creativity.

Clueless (1995)

Rated PG-13

Directed by Amy Heckerling

Starring Alicia Silverstone, Paul Rudd, Brittany Murphy, Stacey Dash, Donald Faison,
Dan Hedaya, Wallace Shawn, Twink Caplan, Justin Walker

THE PLOT

The economy of teen movies necessitates that our heroine is either
the most popular girl in school or the least. If the plot revolves around
the school's least popular girl, you can bet she'll be getting a makeover in time for the prom. If she's the most popular girl, you can expect her to learn the most important life lesson in all of teen
filmdom—that is, Good Clothes Are Less Important Than a Good
Heart. In *Clueless,* a bubble-yum satire of American teenagers, we
meet Cher (Alicia Silverstone), who's the most popular girl at Beverly
Hills High, which should put her in the running to be the most popular high schooler in the whole United States, not to mention the entire
Western world. Her many outfits are fabulous, if a bit ostentatious—
imagine the Delia's catalogue redone by Dali—but she's still more
than a bit clueless about life. As Cher herself puts it, toward the end of
the film, "I decided I needed a complete makeover, except this time I'd
make over my soul." Cher and her best friend Dionne (Stacey Dash)—
as Cher notes, they "were both named after famous singers of the
past, who now do infomercials"—undertake the rehabilitation of new
girl Tai (Brittany Murphy), transforming her from a shy skater into
Mallrat Barbie. They also play cupid for two of their teachers, assum-
ing, correctly, that no one in love could ever hand out Fs. Meanwhile,
Cher begins, despite herself, to fall for the least likely person ever: her
Nietzsche-studying, flannel-wearing, Counting-Crows-loving, good-
doing ex-stepbrother Josh (Paul Rudd).

Writer-director Amy Heckerling's *Clueless* is a loose and frenetic
adaptation of Jane Austen's novel *Emma.* About her heroine, Austen
wrote: "Emma Woodhouse, handsome, clever, and rich, with a com-

fortable home and happy disposition, seemed to unite some of the best blessings of existence; and had lived nearly twenty-one years in the world with very little to distress or vex her." That goes double for 16-year-old Cher (even the death of her mother from a botched liposuction has left her apparently unfazed). She seems, at the first, the quintessential spoiled brat, but her ditzy, superficial attitude belies a real warmth, imagination, and generosity. As played by Alicia Silverstone (then best known as the girl from those Aerosmith videos), Cher is as funny and buoyant as the star of a classic screwball comedy.

 Bonding Potential: 5

With her mother gone, Cher is Daddy's little princess. But her mom, whose giant portrait dominates the foyer, remains the model for saintly behavior. "To tell you the truth, I haven't seen such good-doing since your mother," her father (Dan Hedaya) reassures her at one point. A successful litigator, he is brusque and intimidating, with some of the film's finest insults, but it's clear he's a doting, involved father. And though Cher comes across as a shallow fashion plate with a penchant for hanging out at the mall, she is a good person with an admirable commitment to self-improvement. When you look beyond the fastidiously applied makeup and the skimpy designer clothes, when you decipher all the slangy pop-culture references, you find a sweet, ebullient young girl with a knack for taking care of people. In some small way, *Clueless* celebrates discovering who you are and what's really important to you. All of this gives us plenty to bond over, including, but not limited to, love, family, and the art of breaking in a new pair of shoes.

69

Hunk Factor: 6

According to Cher, Josh qualifies as "kind of a Baldwin," back when looking anything like a Baldwin brother was a good thing. Donald Faison (*Scrubs*) and Jeremy Sisto (*Six Feet Under*) aren't too hard on the eyes, either.

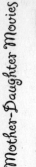

 Hankie Factor: 0

Crying would mess up your makeup, and Cher would have none of that.

Squirming in Your Seat Watching a Sex Scene with Your Mother/Daughter Factor: 0

As virginal—ahem, *hymenally challenged*—Cher puts it, "You see how picky I am about my shoes—and they only go on my feet!"

BEHIND THE SCENES

As Cher is struck by the realization that she loves Josh, the fountains behind her begin to erupt, a moment inspired by the movie *Gigi*.

70

AFTERMATH

Although Alicia Silverstone signed a $10 million deal with Columbia, she never recaptured the success of *Clueless*. She is starring in the TV series *Miss Match,* produced by *Sex in the City*'s Darren Star.

How to Deal (2003)
Rated PG-13

Directed by Clare Kilner

Starring Mandy Moore, Allison Janney, Alexandra Holden, Trent Ford, Peter Gallagher

THE PLOT

Halley (Mandy Moore) hates love. It's no wonder: her parents just got divorced; her disc jockey dad's dating some blonde bimbo; her best friend Scarlett's always off fooling around with her boyfriend Michael; her sister's always getting into fights and making up with her anal-retentive fiancé. Halley, at 17, views love as the first feverish symptom of a disease that always, inevitably, results in a badly damaged heart. Then she meets Macon (Trent Ford), he of the floppy forelocks and thrift store sport coats, and after some lame courting by Macon involving, we kid you not, much use of the Jedi mind trick, they fall into a sweet and gentle "one step forward, two steps back" sort of love affair.

The cardinal sin of women's films, aside from sappiness, is excess. Plots usually consist of an overcrowded series of Big Life Events worthy of a year's subscription to *Soap Opera Digest,* and *How to Deal* is no different. There is, by our count, at the end of the film: two new marriages, two new boyfriends, one dead teenager, one new baby, one life-altering car crash, one cathartic haircut, one unsympathetic guidance counselor, and one very stoned grandmother. We are pleased to report, however, that although the movie covers the entirety of Halley's junior year of high school, there is *no* debilitatingly awkward or sappily unbearable prom scene. But amid all the wedding toasts and eulogies and moronic stepmoms, there is a very small, very touching story about a girl who learns to love and, in surrendering herself to someone else, becomes her own person. Singer Mandy Moore tried hard to be edgy and cynical but is overwhelmed by her formidable cuteness. Still, she is really very good as an obstinate and vulnerable girl opening up to life.

71

♥ Bonding Potential: 9

Divorce is hard on any family. That in no time at all, Halley's dad (Peter Gallagher) moves on to a high-profile romance with his radio cohost makes things all the worse. Her mom (Allison Janney) is reeling, and Halley, like so many teenagers in this situation, is hurt, angry, and confused. A disconnect begins to form between the two women, and as it grows ever wider, each loses sight of what the other is going through. Just when they need each other the most, they are too involved in their own problems to reach out to each other. Halley is simultaneously hiding things from her mom and seething that she doesn't know what's going on in her life; her mom keeps her own secrets and yet feels achingly isolated. Moms and daughters who've been through divorce will identify; those who haven't will surely sympathize.

 Hunk Factor: 7

Model-turned-actor Trent Ford, dressed as though he had just raided a brat pack estate sale, wins Halley over with his arched eyebrows and low, gravelly voice. It works for us, too. *How to Deal* also features a midlife crisis involving Peter Gallagher, who sports a graying soul patch, if you're into that sort of thing.

 Hankie Factor: 6

As we mentioned earlier, this film is stuffed to the gills with huge, emotional events, but thankfully, it refrains from wallowing in its own melodrama. For everything that it packs in, *How to Deal* maintains a surprisingly light mood.

Squirming in Your Seat Watching a Sex Scene with Your Mother/Daughter Factor: 2

BEHIND THE SCENES

How to Deal is actually based on two separate novels from young adult author Sarah Dessen. One involves two friends dealing with teen pregnancy; the other involves a family in crisis.

AFTERMATH

Mandy Moore, further distinguishing herself from the other pop princesses, followed up *How to Deal* with *Cursed,* the latest horror film from *Scream* team Wes Craven and Kevin Williamson.

Never Been Kissed (1999)

Rated PG-13

Directed by Raja Gosnell
Starring Drew Barrymore, David Arquette, Michael Vartan, Leelee Sobieski, Molly
Shannon, Garry Marshall

THE PLOT

73

Josie Geller (Drew Barrymore) has never really been kissed. A 25-year-old copy editor at a Chicago newspaper, she gets her first assignment as a reporter: go undercover as a 17-year-old student for an exposé on high school life. When she was actually 17, Josie was an ugly duckling with the unfortunate nickname of Josie Grossie, and now undercover, she finds that she's *still* unpopular. She manages to connect only with a fellow nerd, Aldys (Leelee Sobieski), and her English teacher (Michael Vartan). But hanging out with the faculty and the mathletes is definitely not what her boss (Garry Marshall) had in mind, and he threatens to fire her unless she gets in with the cool crowd, and fast. Her slacker brother (David Arquette) helps her out by enrolling in high school as well, telling Josie, "All you need is for one person to think you're cool and you're in." Needless to say, he's popular by lunchtime on his first day (kids just can't resist a champion coleslaw eater), and it's only a matter of time before Josie finds herself the oldest prom queen in history.

If you're one of those people who barely survived high school the first time, you might have fantasies about going back and getting it right. We know we do. When Josie's gym teacher tells her that she'll never get into college if she fails gym, she answers back, "You guys are still telling that lie?"

FYI: Cameron Crowe, while a reporter at *Rolling Stone*, did exactly what Josie does to research *Fast Times at Ridgemont High*.

 Bonding Potential: 8

Besides graduating, the best way to get through high school is to talk about it. It's cathartic to watch movies that put in perspective such high school horrors as the prom, Friday pop quizzes, and that elusive phenomenon known as being popular. *Never Been Kissed* shows, among other things, that popularity isn't all it's cracked up to be.

 Hunk Factor: 5

Alias star Michael Vartan was born in France, so that's one in their column, huh?

 Hankie Factor: 0

Squirming in Your Seat Watching a Sex Scene with Your Mother/Daughter Factor: 2

There's a sex ed class scene that might be a little much for very young viewers.

BEHIND THE SCENES

Real-life high school dropout Drew Barrymore was the executive producer, which makes it all the more admirable that she makes herself look so convincingly and mortifyingly geeky.

74

AFTERMATH

Who do we have to pay to keep Garry Marshall *behind* the camera? They probably needed a special trailer for his teeth.

The Princess Diaries (2001)
Rated G

Directed by Garry Marshall
Starring Julie Andrews, Anne Hathaway, Heather Matarazzo, Caroline Goodall,
Mandy Moore, Erik von Detten, Robert Schwartzman

THE PLOT

Fifteen-year-old Mia (Anne Hathaway) is awkward and nerdy. She wears glasses, has frizzy hair, and stinks at team sports. She has a best friend, Lilly (Heather Matarazzo), whose older brother, Michael (Robert Schwartzman), has a crush on her. Mia, however, is attracted to jock jerk Josh (Erik von Detten), who is going out with a cheerleader, Lana (Mandy Moore). In the beginning, it's just business as usual in the complicated romantic entanglements of high schoolers.

Mia lives with her single mother, Helen (Caroline Goodall), in a renovated San Francisco firehouse. She never knew her father, but after his death, she learns he was crown prince of Genovia, a principality between France and Spain. Since Mia is the only blood descendant to the throne, Queen Clarisse (Julie Andrews) comes to town and has only three weeks to teach Mia etiquette *and* to convince her to take over her royal duties. Mia must make a decision—become Princess of Genovia or remain just a normal American teenager.

Haven't we all, at one time or another, harbored a fantasy that somehow we are descended from royalty? No? Well, you can't deny that you've had a fantasy that a world-famous stylist devotes hours to plucking your eyebrows, cutting your hair, doing your makeup, and

75

giving you a new wardrobe, thereby making you a celebrity in your own city.

 Bonding Potential: 9

As Mia gets caught up in the headiness of discovering she's a princess and a beauty, it's her mom who keeps her centered. Grandma may be a queen, dripping in diamonds—and may even resemble Mary Poppins—but it's Mia's mother who has instilled in her all the values that would make her a good leader. Mia even forgives her mother for dating one of her teachers (pickings being slim in San Francisco) and for creating some pretty bad art.

76

HOW DOES JULIA STILES GET SO LUCKY?

1. Heath Ledger, *10 Things I Hate About You*

2. Freddy Prinze Jr., *Down to You*

3. Mekhi Phifer and Josh Hartnett, *O*

4. Matt Damon, *The Bourne Identity*

5. Sean Patrick Thomas, *Save the Last Dance for Me*

6. Ethan Hawke, *Hamlet*

7. Topher Grace, *Mona Lisa Smile*

Hunk Factor: 3

The so-called hunk, Josh, doesn't do that much for us, but the mop-topped Michael is a cutie and he wins this year's Ringo Starr look-alike award.

 Hankie Factor: 0

 Squirming in Your Seat Watching a Sex Scene with Your Mother/Daughter Factor: 0

Are you kidding? It's rated G, and it's not even animated.

BEHIND THE SCENES

A few years prior to shooting, Julie Andrews had throat surgery to remove a nodule on her vocal cords. She sued for medical malpractice when it became evident that the surgery had destroyed her singing voice.

AFTERMATH

Anne Hathaway is currently pursuing a degree from Vassar College, filming movies on breaks.

Sixteen Candles (1984)

Rated PG

Directed by John Hughes
Starring Molly Ringwald, Anthony Michael Hall, Michael Schoeffling, Blanche Baker

THE PLOT

Samantha (Molly Ringwald) is having a rotten sweet sixteen. Her beautiful, selfish older sister (Blanche Baker) is getting married tomorrow to an unbelievable sleazeball and her house is overrun with annoying relatives. Worse yet, every single one of them, even her grandparents, has forgotten that today is her birthday. And things at school aren't much better. Jake Ryan (Michael Schoeffling), Sam's lust object, doesn't even know she's alive. To make matters worse, everywhere she goes, she's hounded by her only suitor, Farmer Ted (Anthony Michael Hall), the relentless and relentlessly irritating King of All Freshman Geeks. Hall plays the geek-like Clark Gable trapped in the prepubescent body of Bill Gates, and Molly Ringwald is never so lovely as she is when completely consumed by self-pity.

Even though kids have been born, graduated from high school, and voted in statewide elections all in the nineteen years since this movie was first released, *Sixteen Candles* still holds up pretty well. Nowadays, most teen movies seem like J. Crew catalogues set to music; they are far less interested in who kids are than in selling them on how they are supposed to be. It's no surprise, then, that a lot of us keep going back to John Hughes, whose mid-eighties comedies were almost as influential on the genre as Shakespeare's great tragedies were on Western drama. Despite its fairy-tale ending, *Sixteen Candles* gets teens right, zits and all. Thus, the jokes in *Sixteen Candles* that might seem awfully offensive (the incessant mockery of a foreign exchange student, for instance) are actually just a teenager's way of kidding around. Likewise, Hughes has a generous sense of teens' turbulent emotional lives, which are often as much in flux as their weird, sprouting puberty-prone bodies. His actors weren't closely shaven

30-year-olds, and so you believed in them and felt for them: sorted cruelly into high school castes, hugely misunderstood, wanting to fit in and to stand out, and falling, every other day, sincerely, seriously, passionately, and completely in love.

 ### Bonding Potential: 7

Since teen angst wasn't invented during the Reagan administration, watching *Sixteen Candles* will help moms remember their own awkward teenage years and give daughters some perspective on their tribulations. The film may establish enough common ground (however temporarily) to curtail those arguments that begin with "Mom, you just don't understand me!"

 ### Hunk Factor: 8

Jake Ryan is downright dreamy, and says things like, "Shit, I've got Caroline in the bedroom right now, passed out cold. I could violate her ten different ways if I wanted to. . . . But I want a serious girlfriend. Somebody I can love that's gonna love me." Who could resist that?

Hankie Factor: 0

Most everyone will sympathize with Sam's plight, but unless the film's eighties wardrobe brings back memories of unfortunate fashion choices, your eyes should remain dry.

Squirming in Your Seat Watching a Sex Scene with Your Mother/Daughter Factor: 2

Sixteen Candles features some teen movie mainstays—boob shot of the hottest girl in school, some graphic sex talk—but is pretty tame by today's *American Pie* standards. In terms of onscreen action, there's not much more than a chaste kiss at the end.

BEHIND THE SCENES

According to *Premiere,* "[Norman] Rockwell's painting of a young girl staring at herself in a mirror inspired the director to cast Molly Ringwald because of her lanky, freckle-faced, Rockwell quality." And so an eighties teen icon was born.

AFTERMATH

Sadly, Molly's transition to adult star has not been a terribly successful one. She did, at age 35, give birth to a baby girl, Matilda, in October 2003.

She's All That (1999)
Rated PG-13

Directed by Robert Iscove
Starring Rachael Leigh Cook, Freddie Prinze Jr., Kieran Culkin, Paul Walker, Jodi Lyn
O'Keefe, Matthew Lillard, Anna Paquin, Kevin Pollak

THE PLOT

Zack (Freddie Prinze Jr.) is popular, handsome, and the third smartest guy in his senior class. Did we mention that he's a star athlete, too? *She's All That* opens with Zack being dumped by his girlfriend, the equally popular Taylor (Jodi Lyn O'Keefe), for Brock Hudson (Matthew Lillard), a cast member of *The Real World* and such a narcissist that he has a tattoo of himself on his arm. So who's Zack going to take to the prom? He makes a bet with his jock friend Dean (Paul Walker) that he can transform, Pygmalion style, the school nerd, Laney (Rachael Leigh Cook), into a prom queen. Laney, an angry art student type, is intense (she assembles collages from photos of starving children) and lives with her father (Kevin Pollak) and younger brother (Kieran Culkin). When Zack asks Laney out, she asks him if he's doing it because he's in a dork outreach program. Still, they connect, and with the aid of Zack's younger sister (Anna Paquin), Laney's makeover begins. Laney and Zack fall for each other, even though Taylor wants to reconcile with Zack and Dean is pursuing Laney. The prom gets closer.

The eyeglasses are the first to go, of course, then the split ends, and finally the paint-splattered clothes. And what movie makeover would be complete without the obligatory eyebrow-plucking scene (see *Moonstruck, Now, Voyager,* and *The Princess Diaries*)? Here come the contact lenses, the new hairdo and wardrobe, the high heels. Voilà! Audrey Hepburn! No, no, we mean Rachael Leigh Cook.

A pop-culture question: Do students in Southern California really wear sports bras to class?

 Bonding Potential: 8

Laney's mother has died of cancer a few years earlier. In the strongest scene in the movie, Laney talks about what it was like to lose her mother.

 Hunk Factor: 10

Tall and handsome, Freddie Prinze Jr. has washboard abs and a really intriguing scar on his face.

 Hankie Factor: 2

Squirming in Your Seat Watching a Sex Scene with Your Mother/Daughter Factor: 2

There is a hilarious scene when Taylor and Brock are in bed. She is trying desperately to seduce him, but he keeps complaining about the smell of her spit on his chest. Another scene that is squirmable, more by its sheer grossness, involves pubic hair in the school cafeteria.

BEHIND THE SCENES

Freddie Prinze Sr. (father of Freddie Jr.) was a big TV star (*Chico and the Man*) in the 1970s who died of a self-inflicted gunshot wound at the height of his fame. He was 22, and his son was only nine months old.

AFTERMATH

Sarah Michelle Gellar, who would later become the real-life wife of Freddie Prinze Jr., makes a brief cameo in the cafeteria scene.

OLDER TEENS ONLY

Election (1999)
Rated R

Directed by Alexander Payne
Starring Matthew Broderick, Reese Witherspoon, Chris Klein, Jessica Campbell, Molly Hagen, Delaney Driscoll

THE PLOT

Mr. McAllister (Matthew Broderick), a dedicated high school teacher and adviser, has an ill-concealed loathing and a little lust for Tracy Flick (Reese Witherspoon), a pert, overachieving schemer who wears rollers to bed. She is running unopposed for student council president when Mr. McAllister convinces a popular jock, Paul (Chris Klein), to run against her. Paul's candidacy infuriates Tracy, and his younger sister, Tammy (Jessica Campbell), who's angry that her lesbian lover is now dating her brother, decides to run for president as well. Mr. McAllister, married for eight years to Diane (Molly Hagen), finds himself attracted to single mom Linda (Delaney Driscoll), whose husband got fired from the school because it was discovered that he was having an affair with . . . Tracy Flick!

A not-too-bright frat type running against a smug know-it-all . . . hmmm, why does the election in *Election* sound vaguely familiar? In many ways, this movie is more like grown-up life than high school.

 ## Bonding Potential: 8

Is there a better way for a mother and daughter to bond than to share a mutual loathing of the kid in class who waves his or her arm frantically with *just* the right answer? We all hate the hall monitor and the hall monitor's equally pushy mom. (Tracy's mom even writes to Connie Chung for career tips for her daughter.) Tracy is the worst kind of goody-goody, the type that has an affair with a married teacher but still wears prim little sweater vests. She is so self-satisfied that it doesn't occur to her that she's unpopular—not even when a fellow student cries out, "Eat me!" during her speeches. Talk about not being able to take a hint.

 ## Hunk Factor: 3

Chris Klein in his pre–*American Pie* incarnation.

 ## Hankie Factor: 0

Squirming in Your Seat Watching a Sex Scene with Your Mother/Daughter Factor: 2

The brief scenes of sexual encounters are played more for humor than for anything else.

BEHIND THE SCENES

Alexander Payne went to his native Omaha for inspiration, though some Omaha residents thought he was poking fun at them here and in *About Schmidt.*

AFTERMATH

Director Payne predicted that Reese Witherspoon was going to be a big star. He was right.

Fast Times at Ridgemont High (1982)
Rated R

Directed by Amy Heckerling
Starring Sean Penn, Jennifer Jason Leigh, Judge Reinhold, Phoebe Cates, Forest Whitaker, Brian Backer, Robert Romanus

84

THE PLOT

Fast Times at Ridgemont High was one of the first teen movies made expressly for teenagers. Previously, teen films were basically nostalgia fests for grown-ups à la *American Graffiti,* but *Fast Times,* a hilarious and surprisingly realistic look at Southern California high schoolers, paved the way for everything from *The Breakfast Club* to *My So-Called Life* to *American Pie.* Director Amy Heckerling juggles a large cast of characters: Stacy (Jennifer Jason Leigh) is a freshman, eager to lose her virginity; her brother Brad (Judge Reinhold), a senior, endures a series of humiliating service industry jobs; Linda (Phoebe Cates) is Stacy's best friend and a self-proclaimed expert on sex; Mark Ratner (Brian Backer) has a crush on Stacy, who has a crush on his sleazy friend Damone (Robert Romanus). Sean Penn, as surfer dude Spicoli, is the most talented actor in a movie teeming with talented young actors; the serious thespian transformed completely and utterly into a righteous stoner beach bum. Spicoli has become a pop culture icon and all his best lines, including "People on 'ludes should not drive," are still often quoted some twenty odd years later.

Writer Cameron Crowe was a 22-year-old *Rolling Stone* reporter when he went undercover to research high school life. He posed for a year as a high school senior in So-Cal, putting his observations into a book that was quickly adapted into this movie. For a Hollywood project, it feels almost like a documentary assembled by some high school AV club to show just among themselves. It's a classic, colorful, honest, and hilarious.

Bonding Potential: 7

Fast Times deals extensively with teenage sex and its consequences. Studio censors hacked up the film's two sex scenes, fearing they were close to porn. What Heckerling had actually done was deliver a ringing endorsement of teen abstinence. Stacy, at 15, loses her virginity to a 26-year-old stereo salesman in a baseball dugout. The encounter is, to say the least, difficult and uncomfortable to watch— even Stacy has to distance herself by studying the graffiti on the cement wall. Her second sexual experience is even worse. It lasts about a nanosecond. Is this normal? she wonders—and then finds herself pregnant. *Fast Times* will definitely leave mothers and daughters with plenty of things to talk about; no matter what your personal position on premarital sex may be, the film will act as a catalyst for a serious discussion that goes well beyond the birds and the bees.

85

Hunk Factor: 6

It turned out that *Fast Times* was the birthplace of many future hunks, including Anthony Edwards (with hair) and Eric Stoltz, credited only as "Stoner Buds." Nic Cage (under his real name, Nicolas Coppola) lost the part of Spicoli to Sean Penn and landed a role so small that you need to freeze-frame to find him.

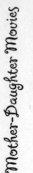 Hankie Factor: 0

Squirming in Your Seat Watching a Sex Scene with Your Mother/Daughter Factor: 8

Moms, be forewarned that *Fast Times at Ridgemont High* earns every bit of its R rating and then some. Particularly squirmworthy is a scene wherein Cates catches Reinhold in the act of, to put it delicately, self-loving.

86

NO EDUCATION IS COMPLETE WITHOUT SEEING

1. *Lawrence of Arabia*

2. *2001: A Space Odyssey*

3. *8½*

4. *Casablanca*

5. *Breathless*

6. *His Girl Friday*

7. *The Wizard of Oz*

8. *Some Like It Hot*

9. *The Sweet Smell of Success*

10. *Marriage, Italian Style*

BEHIND THE SCENES

Heckerling and Crowe searched high and low for the right actor to play Brad; at one point they even asked Sean Penn to switch roles. Heckerling ended up finding the perfect Brad in her real-life neighbor Judge Reinhold. We would be remiss not to mention that he was the casting director's boyfriend. Also, this movie was made in 1982, the same year Jennifer Jason Leigh's father, actor Vic Morrow, was killed in a helicopter crash while making *Twilight Zone: The Movie.*

AFTERMATH

The sexy wife of the biology teacher makes an appearance toward the end of the movie at the high school dance. She was played by Lana Clarkson, an actress who was shot to death in 2003 in Phil Spector's house.

On a lighter note, after making the definitive teen comedy of the eighties, Heckerling went on to direct *Clueless,* the definitive teen comedy of the nineties.

Ghost World (2001)

Rated R

Directed by Terry Zwigoff

Starring Thora Birch, Scarlett Johansson, Steve Buscemi, Brad Renfro, Illeana Douglas, Bob Balaban, Teri Garr

THE PLOT

It's the summer after Enid (Thora Birch) and Rebecca's (Scarlett Johansson) high school graduation. Both Enid and Rebecca start out as misfit teenagers with contempt for the world and all its inhabitants. Speaking of a fellow classmate, Enid says, "I liked her so much better when she was an alcoholic crack addict. She gets in one car wreck and suddenly she's Little Miss Perfect and everyone loves her." But we soon learn that Rebecca's nonconformity is a phase, while Enid's is part of her essence, and over the summer they drift apart. Rebecca starts taking charge of her life while Enid is completely directionless. Enid befriends Seymour (Steve Buscemi), a 40-something mega-nerd who collects vintage records and is a fellow social outcast, telling Rebecca, "He's the opposite of everything I completely hate." As the relationship between Enid and Seymour develops and unravels, she continues to live with her father (Bob Balaban), mostly because she doesn't know where else she would go.

The movie is based on Daniel Clowes's comic book of the same name, and many of the characters, particularly the male characters, resemble guys who are too old to work in the comic book store. *Ghost World* reveals its humanity through a veil of irony, contempt, and sarcasm. It is dark humor almost at its darkest (surpassed only by *Welcome to the Dollhouse*), but is also a look into the rarefied coming of age of a true individual.

 Bonding Potential: 5

Enid's mother is not in residence and we suspect she's dead, although it's not explained. Her father announces that his annoying girlfriend (Teri Garr) is moving in. Enid sobs.

For the poor mothers dealing with teenagers in the throes of rebellion, there is no bonding potential anywhere. But for those who are on the other side of that hideous time of life, this movie could be the bridge that sparks conversation about awkwardness and alienation.

 Hunk Factor: 1

Director Terry Zwigoff reports that his wife told him that Steve Buscemi is the only man he shouldn't leave her alone with.

Hankie Factor: 0

There aren't any hankie-inducing scenes here except for those viewers mourning the lost misery of adolescence.

Squirming in Your Seat Watching a Sex Scene with Your Mother/Daughter Factor: 3

Although there is no sex scene shown in this movie, there is a before-and-after-the-act scene.

BEHIND THE SCENES

The character of Seymour is based in part on director Terry Zwigoff. Like Seymour, Zwigoff is an avid collector of 1920s jazz and blues records. Sophie Crumb, daughter of Robert Crumb, the subject of Zwigoff's previous film, did the drawings in Enid's sketchbook.

AFTERMATH

Brad Renfro was originally supposed to have a bigger part but landed on the proverbial cutting-room floor after Buscemi's comic genius took over the movie. After *Ghost World*, Thora Birch, who looks like a real person, went the way of all starlets by becoming an Atkins diet disciple and getting really skinny. We loved her just the way she was.

89

Heathers (1989)

Rated R

Directed by Michael Lehmann

Starring Winona Ryder, Christian Slater, Shannen Doherty, Lisanne Falk, Kim Walker,
Penelope Milford

THE PLOT

The title refers to a powerful high school clique, comprised of Heather Chandler (Kim Walker), Heather Duke (Shannen Doherty), Heather McNamara (Lisanne Falk), and Veronica (Winona Ryder), a newcomer to the group. The Heathers are popular, sadistic, and enthusiastic about croquet. Veronica, once thrilled to have been adopted by the Heathers, is becoming increasingly horrified by their behavior. She falls for the mysterious new kid in school, JD (Christian Slater), and confesses to him that she doesn't like her friends. Rebellious JD agrees, "Good, I don't like them either," and the two team up to wage war against the Heathers and the high school jocks. Veronica discovers that ID is taking this war literally and goes to unexpected extremes.

90

If ever a movie was a black comedy, it is *Heathers*. It will prove particularly gratifying for those of us who harbored homicidal urges against the bitchy, popular girls in high school. You know who you are.

![hearts] Bonding Potential: 5

Moms, take advantage of the education about high schools and peer pressure that *Heathers* offers. The popular kids are so, well, grown up in their cruelty that we feel little emotion when Veronica and JD wipe them out, a massacre best summarized by Veronica when she says, "My teenage angst bullshit now has a body count."

On a less spectacular level, Veronica has a true *Reviving Ophelia* moment when she bemoans using her high IQ to "figure out what kind of lip gloss to wear." In *Heathers,* the adults—parents and teachers—are idiots. The dads somehow manage to out-dumb the moms, as evidenced by this exchange with Veronica and her father:

> *Veronica*: All we want is to be treated like human beings, not to be experimented on like guinea pigs or patronized like bunny rabbits.
> *Veronica's Dad*: I don't patronize bunny rabbits!

 Hunk Factor: 4

Even though he's shamelessly ripping off Jack Nicholson, we still like Christian Slater.

 Hankie Factor: 0

 Squirming in Your Seat Watching a Sex Scene with Your Mother/Daughter Factor: 2

BEHIND THE SCENES

The original screenplay had a different ending in which the entire school is destroyed and the last scene is a prom of ghosts.

AFTERMATH

This was the beginning of big careers and big trouble for Winona Ryder and Christian Slater.

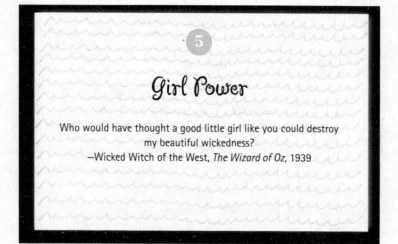

5

Girl Power

Who would have thought a good little girl like you could destroy
my beautiful wickedness?
—Wicked Witch of the West, *The Wizard of Oz*, 1939

Sugar and spice and everything nice? Guess again. Girls have been a force to be reckoned with ever since a tough broad named Cleopatra ruled a civilization, went to war, frolicked with Julius Caesar *and* Mark Antony, and still managed to find time to invent eyeliner. Girl power, like PMS, has been around since the Iron Age, but it's only in recent years that society finally put a name to it. And even if we hadn't, there are tons of movies that celebrate the strong, independent woman. What's better than a flick where the girls are tough and unrepentant: cool, confident women who stop traffic, break hearts, and run the show?

Amélie (2001)

Rated R

Directed by Jean-Pierre Jeunet
Starring Audrey Tautou, Mathieu Kassovitz, Rufus, Yolande Moreau

THE PLOT

A forgotten cache of childhood collectibles finding its way to its now-aged owner? A long-lost love letter from a philandering husband? A globe-trotting garden gnome? Welcome to the world of Amélie Poulain (Audrey Tautou), a shy café waitress who seems to have one foot in Paris and one foot on a cloud. After her mother's untimely (and darkly comedic) death, Amélie is raised by her cold fish of a father (Rufus), a physician, who gives her no physical affection and touches her only during annual checkups. As a result, this small, clinical exchange causes her heart to beat uncontrollably, prompting Papa Poulain to diagnose her with a heart condition and to shield her from all forms of excitement. Little Amélie retreated into the vivid world of her imagination, and she still seems to be a card-carrying citizen there when we catch up with her as a young woman. Grown-up Amélie, still lonely and alone, is a mischievous, impish pixie who takes it upon herself to surreptitiously bring happiness to others, deriving a fair amount of pleasure from her random and intricately orchestrated acts of kindness. Amélie's final and most elaborate scheme is designed to bring her closer to Nino (Mathieu Kassovitz), her unwitting paramour; part treasure hunt and part wild-goose chase, her courtship of Nino is as charming as it is disquieting.

Director Jean-Pierre Jeunet's Paris, filled with rich colors and accordion music, is a lavish dreamscape that serves as the perfect backdrop for Amélie's devilish antics. American movies have long idealized Paris as a romantic playground, but no Hollywood director could ever imbue the city with as much lovely magic as Jeunet does.

94

Bonding Potential: 7

Most movies about love are either saccharine romantic comedies starring chemistry-deprived leads or tragic romances that end with a leaden thud (see *William Shakespeare's Romeo & Juliet*). But this Gallic fable has an infectious and confectionary view of romance: here, love is powerful, playful, wildly inventive, completely transforming. *Amélie* really is irrepressibly charming, a luminous cartoon, and it will take the utmost self-control not to head straight to the airport for a mother-daughter trip to Paris.

 Hunk Factor: 7

Amélie falls for the mysterious loner Nino, who is quiet and darkly handsome; when she sees him, she melts, literally, to the ground. Ooh-la-la.

95

 Hankie Factor: 3

Jeunet lovingly populates his film with an assortment of quirky characters, all of them troubled and lonesome in their own right. They are as sad as Cinderella at the start of her fairy tale. But you'll be quite touched to see Amélie, the fairy godmother, in their midst, bringing them happiness.

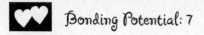 Squirming in Your Seat Watching a Sex Scene with Your Mother/Daughter Factor: 5

Amélie's sexual content earned the film an R rating here in the States, but it is altogether innocent and brief. No wonder the French think we're prudes.

BEHIND THE SCENES

Amélie was a real departure for director Jeunet and star Kassovitz. Kassovitz came to prominence as the director of the edgy, politically charged film *Hate* and Jeunet was the dark visionary behind *Delicatessen* and *City of Lost Children*. What a surprise to receive this valentine from them.

AFTERMATH

The movie was a critical and commercial success in France, but its homogeneous, digitally perfected Paris garnered some criticism and became a politicized debate. Ultimately, both France's president and its prime minister spoke out in support of the crowd-pleaser.

96

Charlie's Angels (2000)
Rated PG-13

Directed by McQ

Starring Cameron Diaz, Drew Barrymore, Lucy Liu, Bill Murray, Sam Rockwell, Kelly Lynch, Tim Curry, the voice of John Forsythe

THE PLOT

Based on the popular seventies TV series, *Charlie's Angels* is a bouncy and irresistibly self-aware action comedy about three gorgeous grown-up Nancy Drews. The Angels still take their orders from the disembodied voice of their mysterious benefactor Charlie, and their ostensible troop leader is still Bosley (Bill Murray, playing, well, Bill Murray), although they spend more time helping him out of jams than he does giving them any sort of guidance. The Angels in the original show were basically walking swimsuit calendars, but these girls—goofy blonde Natalie (Cameron Diaz), boy-crazy redhead Dylan (Drew Barrymore), and tough brunette Alex (Lucy Liu)—are not only beautiful but bad-ass: They race cars, dress in all sorts of sexy and silly disguises, and most important, take no prisoners. It would be hard to overstate how much butt these girls kick. At one point, Natalie even takes on a room full of attackers while setting up a date on her cell phone.

In this outing, the girls are hired to rescue a software mogul (Sam Rockwell) from the clutches of his rival (Tim Curry). Meanwhile, the three operatives of the Charles Townsend Detective Agency juggle the demands of romance, work, and being generally pretty fabulous.

This movie is not going to change anyone's life, but it is like a ride at an amusement park. It's fun while it lasts, and when it's over, you can't remember a thing about it except that you enjoyed it.

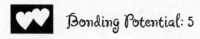 Bonding Potential: 5

Anything boys can do, girls can do better. Not just better, but faster, sexier, and smarter, too. That's the idea of neofeminism in *Charlie's Angels*, and well, you could do quite a lot worse. Moreover, the film treasures female friendship above all.

 Hunk Factor: 6

Luke Wilson, Matt LeBlanc, Sam Rockwell, LL Cool J, and . . . Tom Green? Hey, wait a minute.

Hankie Factor: 0

Leave your hankies where they are; you won't need them for this one.

Squirming in Your Seat Watching a Sex Scene with Your Mother/Daughter Factor: 0

There is one scene in which Dylan has a romp, but it is not explicit at all and she emerges wearing a dress made from a sheet.

BEHIND THE SCENES

It would probably take another whole book to detail all the movie references in *Charlie's Angels,* among them *Ferris Bueller's Day Off, Urban Cowboy, True Lies, West Side Story, The Great Escape, Caddyshack, The Shining, Bullitt, Viva Las Vegas, Putney Swope,* and *Boogie Nights.* Drew Barrymore even revisits her old house from *E.T. The Extra-Terrestrial* when she drops in on two kids playing video games.

AFTERMATH

98

The 2003 sequel, *Charlie's Angels 2: Full Throttle,* cost more money and made less money and far less sense.

Crouching Tiger, Hidden Dragon (2000)
Rated PG

Directed by Ang Lee
Starring Chow Yun-Fat, Michelle Yeoh, Zhang Ziyi, Chang Chen, Cheng Pei-Pei

THE PLOT

Preface: The expression "Crouching tiger, hidden dragon," from Chinese mythology, is about hiding your strength from others.

In ancient China, a great warrior, Li Mu Bai (Chow Yun-Fat), is retiring his famous sword, the Green Destiny. He asks fellow martial artist

Shu Lien (Michelle Yeoh), with whom he shares a deep, unspoken love, to take the sword to Beijing. In Beijing, she meets a young, aristocratic bride-to-be, Jen (Zhang Ziyi), who tells Shu Lien how much she envies her her freedom as an unmarried woman and a warrior. When the sword is stolen, Li Mu Bai suspects that Jade Fox (Cheng Pei-Pei), the woman who killed his master, is responsible. He and Shu Lien unite to retrieve the Green Destiny. On the eve of her wedding Jen gets a visit from Lo (Chang Chen), and a flashback tells their story. The plot and subplots and sub-subplots all lend themselves to breathtaking martial arts sequences featuring women as much as, if not more than, men.

A Note to Mothers: Your daughters are going to want to see the

DREW'S DOS

Match Drew Barrymore's hairdo with the movie.

1. Stringy, black
2. Short, curly, blonde
3. Short, straight, blonde
4. Long, straight, dark brown
5. Short, curly, red
6. Long, straight, light brown
7. Long, wavy, red
8. Blonde ponytail

a. *Charlie's Angels*
b. *Ever After*
c. *Home Fries*
d. *Wedding Singer*
e. *Confessions of a Dangerous Mind*
f. *E.T.*
g. *Riding in Cars with Boys*
h. *Irreconcilable Differences*

Answers: 1.(g) 2.(f) 3.(d) 4.(e) 5.(c) 6.(b) 7.(a) 8.(h)

dubbed version of *Crouching Tiger, Hidden Dragon*. Don't give in: This is a perfect time to introduce them to subtitles, since it's an action movie and so visual.

 Bonding Potential: 10

Jen has three mothers: her real one, a nattering society type; the witchy Jade Fox; and the heroic Shu Lien. Jen rebels against all three. Ancient Chinese noblewomen warriors were teenagers once, too.

Director Ang Lee described *Crouching Tiger, Hidden Dragon* as "Bruce Lee meets Jane Austen." At one point, Shu Lien, sounding just like Elinor Dashwood, acknowledges her secret love of Li Mu Bai, admitting that "to repress one's feelings only makes them stronger." Like the Bennet sisters in *Pride and Prejudice* and the Dashwood sisters in *Sense and Sensibility*, the three women at the center of *Crouching Tiger* are confronted with the limits that society puts on their freedom. But unlike the Austen ladies, these girls are schooled in martial arts, a training that gives them formidable powers. When we saw *Crouching Tiger, Hidden Dragon* at the movies, the audience broke into spontaneous applause after the first breathtaking martial arts sequence . . . with two women!

Hunk Factor: 7

It's about time Asian guys came into their hunk heritage. Jet Li might be the most famous hottie (with apologies to nonhunk Jackie Chan), but *Crouching Tiger* introduced us to Chow Yung-Fat. Here's a guy with the word *fat* in his name and he's still sexy! But our very favorite hunk was Chang Chen as the desert bandit, Lo. Sigh.

Hankie Factor: 6

The hankie factor is augmented by Yo Yo Ma's heartbreaking cello solos.

BEHIND THE SCENES

The part of Li Mu Bai was originally offered to Jet Li, but he made *Romeo Must Die* instead. Chow Yung-Fat, Michelle Yeoh, and Cheng Pei-Pei are all veterans of Hong Kong action movies. When drama student and dancer Zhang Ziyi signed on, however, she was so young that she needed written permission from her school to be in the movie.

AFTERMATH

Ang Lee won the Academy Award for best director and should have won for best picture.

Dick (1999)
Rated PG-13

Directed by Andrew Fleming

Starring Kirsten Dunst, Michelle Williams, Dan Hedaya, Will Ferrell, Bruce McCulloch, Dave Foley, Ana Gasteyer, Harry Shearer, Saul Rubinek

THE PLOT

Pink polyester pantsuits, political intrigue, and lots of laughs. What more could you want? Betsy (Kirsten Dunst) and Arlene (Michelle Williams) are two adorable, giggly teenage girls who always seem to be in the right place at the right time to explain all of the missing pieces of information from the Watergate scandal. Guess who's the real Deep Throat? Guess what happened to those eighteen minutes of missing tape? Guess who really brought down the Nixon presidency?

Betsy and Arlene are sneaking out to mail their entry to a "Win a

Date with Bobby Sherman" contest when they stumble upon G. Gordon Liddy in the midst of the Watergate break-in. To keep them quiet, Nixon (Dan Hedaya) ends up making the girls the official White House dog walkers for Checkers and secret teen advisers to the president. Needless to say, it's only a matter of time before all the Bobby Sherman posters come down and Arlene is doodling "Mrs. Arlene Nixon" in her school notebook.

Dunst and Williams are perfection, and the supporting cast is a delight. Will Ferrell and *Kids in the Hall*'s Bruce McCulloch play reporters Woodward and Bernstein as vain, preening idiots. Hedaya creates a caricature of Nixon that is at once hilarious and touchingly pitiful. Hedaya is the master of the one-liner and his "Checkers, shut up—or I'll feed you to the Chinese!" will have you laughing for days to come. Andrew Fleming's comedy *Dick* is an absolute ball.

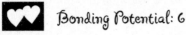 Bonding Potential: 6

102

Director Andrew Fleming and cowriter Sheryl Longin reinvent the Watergate scandal as a wicked, giddy farce, but *Dick* doesn't trivialize history at all. Sure, if you want your daughter to learn about Nixon's downfall, it's still better for her to pick up a history book or even rent *All the President's Men*. *Dick* is, in fact, less factual than even your average *Saturday Night Live* sketch (although it has a good deal more humor). But if you want your daughter to learn about how it *felt* to live through Watergate, you couldn't do better than *Dick*. It is often said that the Nixon administration was when America lost its innocence; *Dick* explores that idea in the story of two trusting, seemingly ditzy girls whose eyes open to things they never could have imagined. As Betsy and Arlene's crush on Nixon sours, America's disillusionment with him grows.

Once the laughs subside, you're sure to be left with plenty of things to talk about, especially with daughters who lived through the scandals of the Clinton years.

Hunk Factor: 0

Arlene swoons for Tricky Dick (until she learns he really hates his dog), but yeah, no hunks in residence.

 Hankie Factor: 0

 Squirming in Your Seat Watching a Sex Scene with Your Mother/Daughter Factor: 0

BEHIND THE SCENES

Mike Medavoy sent a copy of the script to Nixon White House counsel John Dean, who thought it was "funny and cute" and gave them some ideas. There actually is a place on the real tapes where Nixon yells at (and it sounds as though he kicks) the dog. Dean told them that Nixon had a very troubled relationship with dogs—he had been humiliated in public by them on several occasions.

AFTERMATH

Most of the clothes the girls are wearing are actual garments from the seventies, which means plenty of polyester, a fabric notorious for retaining odors, causing a problem after sixteen hours under the lights.

103

Legally Blonde (2001)

Rated PG-13

Directed by Robert Luketic

Starring Reese Witherspoon, Luke Wilson, Selma Blair, Matthew Davis, Victor Garber,
Jennifer Coolidge

THE PLOT

Beverly Hills sorority girl Elle Woods (Reese Witherspoon) gets dumped by boyfriend Warner Huntington III (Matthew Davis) just before he leaves for Harvard Law School. A woman scorned, Elle wants to prove to him that she's no idiot, so she applies to Harvard Law, too. She is accepted based on her 4.0 average and admissions video, in which she wears a sequined bathing suit. Warner is shocked to see her and her dog Bruiser (in matching outfits) as classes begin at Harvard. Elle, in turn, is equally shocked to discover that he is engaged to the snobby Vivian Kensington (Selma Blair), who immediately becomes Elle's archrival.

It seems that everyone is exposed to prejudice in one form or another. Even though Elle is rich and beautiful, she still faces this put-down from her boyfriend: "If I'm going to be a senator, I need to marry a Jackie, not a Marilyn." No one takes her seriously until she takes *herself* seriously, and when she does, she takes on her ex-boyfriend, Harvard, and finally, the legal system.

Bonding Potential: 5

Elle does have a mother but not much of one—she's sort of a stick figure lounging by the pool with a martini. Elle relates more to another older woman, a working-class manicurist, Paulette (Jennifer Coolidge). As Elle becomes empowered, she likewise empowers Paulette and helps her confront her brutish ex-boyfriend to reclaim her dog. Elle also triumphs over sexual harassment by a smug law professor (Victor Garber) and makes inspired use of her beauty expertise in a courtroom showdown.

We are of the opinion that it's never too early to learn about the horrors of sexual harassment. *Legally Blonde* takes this on in an effective, tasteful way. On a happier note, in the spirit of girlfriends everywhere, former rivals Elle and Vivian eventually join forces.

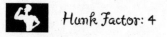 *Hunk Factor:* 4

Luke Wilson is adorable as Elle's law school TA.

105

WAR MOVIES FOR CHICKS

1. *The Thin Red Line*

2. *Three Kings*

3. *Paths of Glory*

4. *Gallipoli*

5. *Saving Private Ryan*

6. *Platoon*

7. *Breaker Morant*

8. *Manchurian Candidate*

9. *Patton*

10. *The Deer Hunter*

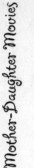

Hankie Factor: 0

Squirming in Your Seat Watching a Sex Scene with Your Mother/Daughter Factor: 0

BEHIND THE SCENES

Reese Witherspoon researched her role by hanging out at the sorority houses at USC and watching shoppers at Barney's. Matthew Davis, who played her shallow ex-boyfriend, claims he did his research by reading a biography of President George W. Bush.

AFTERMATH

Reese Witherspoon earned $2.5 million for this movie, but reportedly earned $15 million for its sequel, *Legally Blonde 2: Red, White & Blonde.*

106

A Little Princess (1995)
Rated G

Directed by Alfonso Cuarón
Starring Liesel Matthews, Eleanor Bron, Liam Cunningham, Rusty Schwimmer,
        Vanessa Lee Chester

THE PLOT

The movie opens in India with 10-year-old Sara (Liesel Matthews) telling stories from a Sanskrit epic. Her widowed father (Liam Cunningham) must leave to fight in World War I, so he brings Sara to America to board at Miss Minchin's Seminary for Girls. Her father departs, telling Sara she is his little princess and that "magic has to be believed to be real." (The movie is based on a book written in 1905, long before calling a female a princess had become a pretty derogatory term.)

It soon becomes evident that the school's headmistress, Miss Minchin (Eleanor Bron), and her sister, Miss Amelia (Rusty Schwimmer), are not the benevolent educators that one would have hoped for. When word comes that Sara's father is dead, Miss Minchin, realizing Sara is now penniless, promptly moves her to the servants' quarters, where she befriends Becky (Vanessa Lee Chester). One day Sara's scarf blows away; she chases after it and finds it at the feet of an Indian man draped in gorgeous colors with a monkey on his shoulder. After this encounter, Sara's spirits return; she starts telling stories again, and the magic begins.

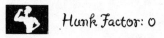 Bonding Potential: 8

Most of the mothers in this story are dead, and sadly, no mom substitutes make an appearance. Rather, it's a story about the love between a father and daughter. This provides an excellent opportunity for moms and daughters to discuss that strange species—men—including the mysterious creature known as Dad. On another note, we see how, in the face of the beastly Miss Minchin, the girls become one another's family. *A Little Princess* is about friendship and loyalty as much as anything else.

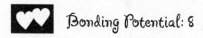 Hunk Factor: 0

There are no hunks in this movie, but there is a lot of romance.

 Hankie Factor: 10

We defy you to stay dry-eyed when Sara comforts her father as he goes off to war, telling him she's going to be fine. Okay, if you survive that, see if you can hold back the waterworks during the ending.

Squirming in Your Seat Watching a Sex Scene with Your Mother/Daughter Factor: 0

BEHIND THE SCENES

Liesel Matthews's parents were undergoing a vicious custody battle while she was making this movie. Mom wanted her to be billed under her last name (Bagley); Dad wanted her to use his name (Pritzker), and even threatened to pull her from the movie. A compromise of sorts was reached when she used her brother's name, Matthew.

AFTERMATH

Liesel Matthews, now a student at Columbia University and heiress to the Hyatt Hotel fortune, continues to have a decidedly un-fairy-tale-like relationship with her parents. In 2003, she brought a lawsuit against Dad, claiming he had bilked her trust fund of $1 billion.

Shadow of a Doubt (1943)
Not rated

Directed by Alfred Hitchcock

Starring Teresa Wright, Joseph Cotten, Macdonald Carey, Hume Cronyn, Henry Travers, Patricia Collinge

THE PLOT

Young Charlie (Teresa Wright) lives in Santa Rosa, a sunny town with clean streets and smiling traffic cops, and she is overcome with teenage ennui. Much to her delight, she learns her namesake, Uncle Charlie (Joseph Cotten), is coming to visit. In time, Charlie discovers that her uncle is the Merry Widow Murderer, a serial killer who seduces and does in rich widows. To make matters worse, there's a pair of detectives hot on Uncle Charlie's trail.

What is most fascinating about *Shadow of a Doubt* is Charlie's relationship to her uncle. She calls it a telepathic connection. We are tempted to call it incest (implied, of course, since this *is* 1943). At one point the virginal Charlie tells her uncle, "We're not just an uncle and a niece. It's something else. I know you . . . I have a feeling that inside you there's something secret and wonderful. I'll find out." Sounds a bit odd, don't you think?

Bonding Potential: 7

Young Charlie is *so* protective of her mother Emma (Patricia Collinge): "Poor Mother, she works like a dog, just a dog. . . . I mean, she's not just a mother. And I think we ought to do something for her." Oh, if only all daughters would give speeches like that! And it is our young, innocent Charlie who is the first and only family member to realize that her uncle is a killer. Summoning up all her strength, Charlie goes into killer mode herself to protect her family, Mom in particular. In the midst of all this action, Charlie's father (Henry Travers) and his nerdy neighbor (Hume Cronyn) are obliviously reading detective magazines and talking about murderers.

Hunk Factor: 2

Cotten is weirdly attractive in a psychopathic way; it helps that you never actually see him kill anyone. Look for his introduction to the movie: His train comes into town belching black smoke, implying, according to François Truffaut, that "the devil was coming to town." Uncle Charlie provides a glimpse into the male misogynist mind in his diatribe against women: "The cities are full of women, middle-aged widows, husbands dead, husbands who've spent their lives making fortunes, working and working. And then they die and leave their money to their wives, their silly wives. And what do the wives do, these useless women? You see them in the hotels. The best hotels, every day by the thousands, drinking the money, eating the money, losing the money at bridge, playing all day and all night, smelling of money, proud of their jewelry but of nothing else, horrible, faded, fat, greedy women. . . . Are they human or are they fat wheezing animals, hmmm? And what happens to animals when they get too fat or too old?" Okay, okay, Uncle Charlie, we get your point.

 Hankie Factor: 0

REPORTED TO BE DIVAS

True or False?

1. Cameron Diaz

2. Frances McDormand

3. Sharon Stone

4. Whoopi Goldberg

5. Lisa Kudrow

6. Halle Berry

7. Drew Barrymore

8. Demi Moore

9. Roseanne

10. Kelly Osborne

Answers: 1.(f) 2.(f) 3.(t) 4.(t) 5.(f) 6.(t) 7.(f) 8.(t) 9.(t) 10.(t)

BEHIND THE SCENES

Hitchcock named Charlie's sainted mother Emma after his own sainted mother, who died during the filming of *Shadow of a Doubt.*

AFTERMATH

Hitchcock's own misogyny (see above speech) reared its ugly head years later: When Melanie Griffith was a little girl (hard to believe there ever was a time, isn't it?), Hitch sent her a miniature coffin with a doll-sized replica of her mother, Tippi Hedren, one of his leading ladies.

The Secret of Roan Inish (1994)
Rated PG

Directed by John Sayles
Starring Jeni Courtney, Eileen Colgan, Mick Lally, John Lynch, Richard Sheridan

THE PLOT

Fiona Conneelly (Jeni Courtney), 10 years old, has recently lost her mother, so she's sent to live with her grandparents (Eileen Colgan and Mick Lally) on the west coast of 1940's Ireland. For generations, Fiona's family lived on a coastal island called Roan Inish, which translated from the Irish, means "island of the seals." The previous year, she and her family had evacuated Roan Inish and in the process, they lost Fiona's infant brother at sea.

Time passes, and Fiona learns the folklore of her family from a slightly daft cousin (John Lynch), who explains that the Conneellys are descendents of a *selkie,* a seal who can turn into a woman. This inspires Fiona and her 13-year-old cousin, Eamon (Richard Sheridan), to keep returning to Roan Inish to learn its secrets and restore it to its former glory.

One of the reasons this is such a perfect family movie is that it doesn't talk down to kids. The narrative unfolds via flashbacks that are a beautiful combination of legend and fact. It's refreshing for adults and children alike to see how magic and mysticism are accepted as part of everyday life in this unique Irish culture. A word of caution: The sight of an infant getting whisked out to sea may disturb the very young. But what girl wouldn't want to be Fiona, taking a nap in the wildflowers under the bluest sky?

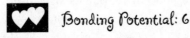 Bonding Potential: 6

Fiona is a little girl who has experienced lots of sadness. She loses her baby brother, then her mother, and even finds out that her grandparents are soon to be evicted. When she realizes that her family must return to Roan Inish, Fiona sets out to make this happen. Moms can, if they choose, identify with the cozy grandmother, but there are any number of seals and a genuine *selkie* who turn out to be pretty maternal as well.

 Hunk Factor: 2

John Lynch is usually cute, but not when he's smeared with mackerel guts.

Hankie Factor: 2

A girl without a mother!

BEHIND THE SCENES

This was a radical departure for the director, whose previous efforts leaned toward gritty realism rather than toward the magic realism of *The Secret of Roan Inish*.

AFTERMATH

This was the first film for its star, Jeni Courtney. She made two more movies, both obscure, and is now a student at Cambridge University.

That Hamilton Woman (1941)
Not rated

113

Directed by Alexander Korda
Starring Vivien Leigh, Laurence Olivier, Alan Mowbray, Gladys Cooper, Sara Allgood

THE PLOT

Young Emma Hart (Vivien Leigh) thinks she has put her racy past behind her when her fiancé sends her and Mom (Sara Allgood) to Naples to meet his uncle, Sir William Hamilton (Alan Mowbray), the British ambassador to Naples. Upon their arrival, Emma finds out that her lover has actually passed her on to the aging uncle. She is understandably distraught, and is convinced by the old man to stay in Naples. In time, she becomes Lady Hamilton and things go quite swimmingly until Lord Horatio Nelson (Laurence Olivier) comes along. Emma helps Nelson in his battle against Napoléon and they fall in love. When Nelson returns to England a hero, Emma accompanies him and meets his battle-axe wife; much drama ensues. After she has his child out of wedlock, Emma learns that Nelson, having returned to war, has died at the Battle of Trafalgar.

We should mention that we are big fans of Vivien Leigh. She is exceptionally beautiful in this movie, and only our Viv can pull off wearing some of those gaudy gowns and phony-looking jewels without looking vulgar.

 ### Bonding Potential: 7

The eighteenth century produced some tough chicks: Emma saves Nelson, the British fleet, and the empire itself when she leans on her girlfriend, the Queen of Naples, for aid. She asks Nelson, "Has it occurred to you that women can sometimes be of more help than men?" Emma's mother is loving but her morals are, to say the least, casual. The old dame trots to Naples with her daughter and pooh-poohs the messy fact that her daughter's boyfriend has pimped her out to his old uncle.

114

 ### Hunk Factor: 9

That Hamilton Woman and *Wuthering Heights* are great ways to introduce today's girls to the sexuality and offbeat handsomeness of Sir Laurence Olivier. He still looks good in *That Hamilton Woman* even after he loses an eye *and* an arm!

 ### Hankie Factor: 7

Lord Nelson's dying words were "Poor Emma." He was right!

Squirming in Your Seat Watching a Sex Scene with Your Mother/Daughter Factor: 0

BEHIND THE SCENES

Laurence Olivier and Vivien Leigh shocked the Hollywood establishment by running off together while they were married to other people. They had appeared together before, but this was the first time they costarred in a movie after they'd become husband and wife. It was also the last time.

AFTERMATH

The movie, part of the war's "Save Britannia" effort, draws parallels between Napoléon and Hitler, so it's not surprising that Winston Churchill saw it eighty-three times. His favorite part was when Nelson shouted, "Look out, Bonaparte, by gad we shall lick you now!"

Whale Rider (2002)
Rated PG-13

115

Directed by Niki Caro
Starring Keisha Castle-Hughes, Rawiri Paratene, Vicky Haughton, Cliff Curtis

THE PLOT

Pai (Keisha Castle-Hughes), now a 12-year-old Maori girl living in coastal New Zealand, lost her mother and twin brother in childbirth. Her father, Porourangi (Cliff Curtis), is next in line to be the chief, an honor he refuses to accept. Instead, Porourangi goes to Europe to be an artist and leaves Pai with her grandparents, Nanny Flowers (Vicky Haughton) and Koro (Rawiri Paratene), the tribal chief. According to tradition, only first-born sons are allowed to be chief. Koro is fiercely traditional and not interested in grooming a girl, even his granddaughter Pai, to be chief. Koro sets up a school for first-born village boys in the hope that one of them will emerge as the next chief. Pai is not allowed to attend the lessons, but she enlists her uncle to help her learn the things the boys are learning. Pai, named after the mythic founder of the tribe, Paikea, is steeped in Maori tradition. She stoically endures her grandfather's anger—she loves him so much that she goes to great lengths for him to understand her. When her strength, courage, and emotion are finally revealed, it is very moving.

Pai knows that she is destined to be the leader of her tribe, even if it puts her in opposition to her beloved grandfather. The movie follows Pai's desire to turn her internal journey into her reality and the audience is with her at every turn. It is the kind of story we have heard before, but Castle-Hughes is convincing and deeply endearing. The filmmakers also stay away from the predictable to bring us a moving, interesting story about a people most of us know little about.

 ### Bonding Potential: 10

This movie takes "standing up for what you believe" to new heights. Pai is a good example for all of us when it comes to truth, honesty, and belief in yourself. It will make us all want to find that strong, wise 12-year-old girl within ourselves and to see her in those we love.

 ### Hunk Factor: 8

Cliff Curtis: More Maoris, please!

 ### Hankie Factor: 10

Forget about the crocodile tears—this one brings on the whale tears.

Squirming in Your Seat Watching a Sex Scene with Your Mother/Daughter Factor: 0

BEHIND THE SCENES

This was Niki Caro's first film, and she won the top prize at the Toronto Film Festival.

AFTERMATH

Keisha Castle-Hughes, discovered in her classroom by the *Whale Rider*'s casting agent, really is of Maori descent. She had never acted before, and in a recent interview claimed she has no intention of ever acting again.

OLDER TEENS ONLY

Aliens (1986)
Rated R

117

Directed by James Cameron
Starring Sigourney Weaver, Carrie Henn, Michael Biehn, Paul Reiser, Lance Henriksen, Bill Paxton, Jenette Goldstein

THE PLOT

This sequel to *Alien* (1979) opens with Ripley (Sigourney Weaver) waking from fifty-seven years of hibernation in space. She is the only survivor of a commercial spacecraft that had been attacked by an alien species. Back on earth, she tells her horror story about the aliens: They are at once slimy and bony, repellent critters with acid coursing through their veins instead of blood. After attacking, they impregnate some of their victims with a refreshing disregard for gender. Only Burke (Paul Reiser), the company man, believes her story.

Much to her chagrin, Ripley learns that humans are now colonizing LV-426, the planet on which her crew discovered the aliens. When contact is lost with LV-426, Ripley and Burke are sent back to investigate. Accompanying them on this "express elevator to hell" is a marine squadron that includes Hicks (Michael Biehn), Hudson (Bill Paxton), Vasquez (Jenette Goldstein), and the android, Bishop (Lance Henriksen). Once on LV-426, they discover its sole survivor, Newt (Carrie Henn), a little girl who appeals to Ripley's maternal side.

Before there was Trinity, before there was Xena, before there was even Oprah, there was Ripley. She's buff and tough and not even a tiny bit butch. While the original *Alien* was about "a haunted house in space," *Aliens* is pure action/adventure, making Ripley filmdom's first female action hero. She battles the aliens as they run amuck (sorry, pun intended) and finally has a battle to the death with the alien queen. She looks great in white cotton underpants too!

 Bonding Potential: 8

The bond between the childless woman and the motherless child makes *Aliens* an action movie with a heart. Before they connect, Ripley is angry and depressed and Newt is traumatized; they find solace in each other. Besides, their relationship gives us a welcome break from the movie's intensity, allowing us to chomp our popcorn without running the risk of needing the Heimlich maneuver. To rescue Newt, Ripley faces off with the queen mother of the aliens. It's dueling single moms—somehow we just *know* the alien queen ain't married either—fighting to save their young, with "Keep away from her, you *bitch*!" becoming Ripley's war cry.

 Hunk Factor: 5

Because of Michael Biehn and Bill Paxton but, sorry, not Paul Reiser. And by the way, is that a rug?

 Hankie Factor: 0

Squirming in Your Seat Watching a Sex Scene with Your Mother/Daughter Factor: 0

Because it's plenty scary and creepy, and definitely not for young children.

BEHIND THE SCENES

Ridley Scott directed the original *Alien*. Its sequel languished until James Cameron, fresh from the success of *The Terminator,* was given the green light to direct this. From here on Cameron's career took off, peaking with *Titanic* and tanking with his *Titanic* Oscar speech. If only the alien queen could come back from the dead to impale him before he made a fool of himself by braying, "I'm King of the World!"

119

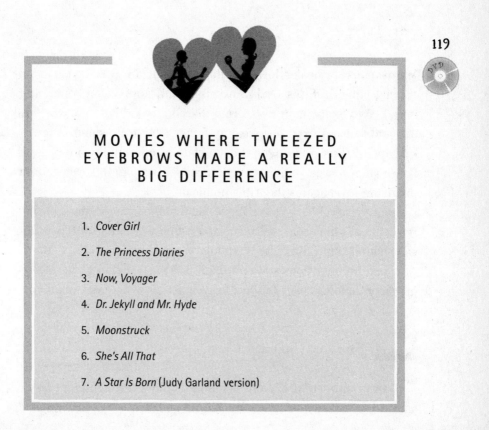

MOVIES WHERE TWEEZED EYEBROWS MADE A REALLY BIG DIFFERENCE

1. *Cover Girl*

2. *The Princess Diaries*

3. *Now, Voyager*

4. *Dr. Jekyll and Mr. Hyde*

5. *Moonstruck*

6. *She's All That*

7. *A Star Is Born* (Judy Garland version)

AFTERMATH

Two totally unnecessary sequels followed *Aliens*. Sigourney Weaver was nominated for an Academy Award for this performance and Paul Reiser went on to *Mad About You*. Carrie Henn, so effective as Newt, never made another movie.

Fargo (1996)
Rated R

Directed by Joel Coen
Starring Frances McDormand, William H. Macy, Steve Buscemi, Harve Presnell, Peter
  Stormare

THE PLOT

Minneapolis car dealer Jerry Lundegaard (William H. Macy) is in a financial jam. He hires Carl (Steve Buscemi) and Gaear (Peter Stormare), two petty gangsters from Fargo, to kidnap his wife and demand ransom from her wealthy father (Harve Presnell). After the kidnapping, Carl and Gaear shoot a state trooper and two witnesses. Police chief Marge Gunderson (Frances McDormand), seven months pregnant, investigates the triple homicide.

Some critics of *Fargo* have suggested that the Coen brothers, former residents of Minnesota, were sticking it to their home state with this snowbound film noir. They certainly weren't making fun of Marge: Although an enormous statue of Paul Bunyan, looking like a bloated psychopath, looms over *Fargo*, Marge emerges as the real folk hero.

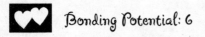 *Bonding Potential:* 6

If an immensely pregnant woman waddling through eight feet of snow to investigate a triple homicide isn't empowering, then we don't know what is. Marge may wear an Elmer Fudd hat, use hokey expressions like "Okey dokey" and "You're dern tootin,'" and chow down at the Radisson buffet, but she's an ace detective. Totally fearless, she approaches a killer as he shovels his partner into a wood chipper, leaving only his foot exposed. She's the film moral center, as evidenced by her speech to the killer at the end of the movie: "There's more to life than a little money, you know. And here you are. And it's a beautiful day."

 Hunk Factor: 0

 Hankie Factor: 0

Squirming in Your Seat Watching a Sex Scene with Your Mother/Daughter Factor: 0

BEHIND THE SCENES

The plot brought the characters to North Dakota because that was where the snow was—Minnesota was experiencing its warmest winter in a hundred years. Joel Coen wrote the part of Marge for his wife, Frances McDormand, prompting her remark, "If people want to say I slept with him for thirteen years to get the part in *Fargo,* let them!" The Coen brothers are uncharacteristically modest for show folk: They edited the film themselves but credited Roderick James, an elusive and quite fictional Englishman. This posed quite a problem when Roderick James was nominated for an Oscar.

AFTERMATH

McDormand won the Oscar for best actress, her husband won for best screenplay, and the wood chipper was a float in a Fourth of July parade in Minnesota.

Run, Lola, Run (1998)

Rated R

Directed by Tom Tykwer

Starring Franka Potente, Moritz Bleibtreu, Herbert Knaup, Nina Petri, Armin Rohde, Joachim Król

THE PLOT

Lola (Franka Potente) gets a call from her boyfriend Manni (Moritz Bleibtreu), who has twenty minutes to come up with 100,000 deutsche marks or gangsters will kill him—it's a race against the clock and Lola takes it on. When she hangs up the phone, she heads out in her Doc Martens to dash for cash across Berlin. We see three versions of her odyssey, each with the same people facing different obstacles and outcomes determined by split-second differences in timing.

122

We don't really know Lola, but we care about her. Lola's desire to save her man imbues her with herculean strength. We feel her desperation and see her devotion and dedication.

The look of the movie is wonderful. Sequences with Lola and Manni are shot on 35 mm film; those scenes without them are shot on video; there is animation, still photography, slow motion, and black-and-white film—all representing different things. Tykwer also includes jump-cutting, handheld cameras, steadi cam, split-screen images, and wonderful aerial shots.

This is a fundamentally urban story yet it moves like a gazelle in the grasslands. *Run, Lola, Run* is about the unforeseeable consequences of seemingly inconsequential decisions. We make hundreds of such decisions every day without thinking that each is potentially life-changing. Tykwer leaves the philosophical ruminations to the viewer, presenting the situation and letting us make sense of it.

Bonding Potential: 6

This movie is an exploration of fate and coincidence. One moment can forever alter everything. Is it destiny? Is it chance? Is it the truth on which the law of the universe is based?

 Hunk Factor: 5

Manni is handsome in a Eurotrash kind of way, but perhaps not hot enough to be running all over creation for.

 Hankie Factor: 0

Squirming in Your Seat Watching a Sex Scene with Your Mother/Daughter Factor: 0

123

BEHIND THE SCENES

The movie emerged from Tykwer's mind with the image of a woman running; then he came up with the title; then he wrote the script. Tykwer not only wrote and directed; he also (with Johnny Klimek and Reinhold Heil) created the hypnotic, insistent techno-pop music that drives everything before it. During shooting, Franka Potente could not wash her hair for seven weeks because the red hair color was very sensitive to water and would have got lighter with every washing.

AFTERMATH

Director and leading lady began a long-term romance.

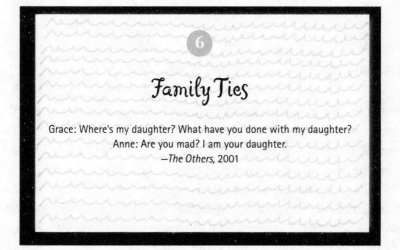

6

Family Ties

Grace: Where's my daughter? What have you done with my daughter?
Anne: Are you mad? I am your daughter.
—*The Others*, 2001

Tolstoy began *Anna Karenina* with the famous line "Happy families are all alike; every unhappy family is unhappy in its own way." Families are provocative, annoying, frustrating, emotionally trying, and to use an exhausted word, dysfunctional. Alas, your family is not an elective relationship: You are genetically bound to those people, so you might as well make the best of it. One approach to this daunting feat is to see how they do it in the movies. You may just find that you wouldn't trade the members of your motley crew for anyone else.

Bend It Like Beckham (2002)

PG-13

Directed by Gurinder Chadha

Starring Parminder K. Nagra, Keira Knightley, Jonathan Rhys-Meyers, Anupam Kher,
Shaheen Khan

THE PLOT

Jess (Parminder K. Nagra) is torn between her love of soccer and the insistence of her traditional Indian parents (Anupam Kher and Shaheen Khan) that she begin to behave "like a proper lady." But Jess, with the help of teammate Jules (Keira Knightley) and coach Joe (Jonathan Rhys-Meyers), is intent on bucking the convention that "Indian girls aren't supposed to play football." Elaborate schemes and madcap adventures ensue, and the result is a charming film that celebrates both women's athletics and Indian culture, proving that the two don't have to be mutually exclusive.

You're still a lot more likely to see women kicking butt on screen than kicking a ball around. Given the paucity of sports films featuring women anyplace but the sidelines, we should consider ourselves lucky for *Bend It Like Beckham*, 2002's joyous celebration of girls out on the soccer pitch. It is all the more remarkable for dealing sweetly and nimbly with issues of family and ethnicity, teen rebellion, young love, female empowerment, and gay acceptance. A massive hit in the UK, *Bend It Like Beckham* is rousing, inspiring fun. You'll laugh your shin guards off.

Bonding Potential: 7

Perhaps the greatest achievement of *Bend It Like Beckham* is the way it treats a modern family's generational rift (in this case immigrant parents and their assimilated children) with honesty and humor. It will speak to mothers and daughters alike.

Hunk Factor: 6

Here in the States, Jonathan Rhys-Meyers should do for soccer coaches what Hugh Grant did for stammering suitors. You'd gladly run drills for him any day.

 Hankie Factor: 0

Bend It Like Beckham is a heartwarming, feel-good movie straight out of the playbook.

 Squirming in Your Seat Watching a Sex Scene with Your Mother/Daughter Factor: 0

Most of the action is on the field, not in the bedroom.

127

BEHIND THE SCENES

According to the *Los Angeles Times*, the film was so wildly popular in New Delhi that its fans formed the "Bend It" soccer league. By the way, the scar on Parminder Nagra's leg is real—the writers worked it into the script.

AFTERMATH

Parminder Nagra's impressive debut in *Bend It Like Beckham* landed her a role on TV's *ER*, and Keira Knightley traded in her cleats for a corset in the swashbuckling adventure *Pirates of the Caribbean: The Curse of the Black Pearl.*

How to Make an American Quilt (1995)
Rated PG-13

Directed by Jocelyn Moorhouse
Starring Winona Ryder, Ellen Burstyn, Anne Bancroft, Maya Angelou, Kate Nelligan,
Jean Simmons, Dermot Mulroney, Kate Capshaw, Johnathon Schaech

THE PLOT

128

Finn (Winona Ryder) is a perennial student, always working on her master's thesis. After her boyfriend Sam (Dermot Mulroney) proposes, she decides to spend the summer with her grandmother (Ellen Burstyn) and great-aunt (Anne Bancroft), who are part of a quilting bee, to mull over his proposal. Anna (Maya Angelou), the leader of the bee, determines the theme of the new quilt will be "Where Love Resides" and decides it will be Finn's wedding quilt whether or not she marries Sam. Since Finn's thesis is about women's tribal activities, this is an excellent opportunity for her to do research by talking to these women and learning about their lives.

Joan Crawford and Bette Davis may be dead, but the woman's movie lives on. Finn grapples with commitment to Sam, asking, "How do you merge into this thing called 'couple' and still keep room for yourself? And how do we know if we're only supposed to be with one person for the rest of our lives?" Good question.

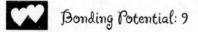 *Bonding Potential*: 9

How to Make an American Quilt begins with Finn's relationship with her grandmother, and when her mother (Kate Capshaw) turns up toward the end of the movie, it becomes the story of three generations of women. Finn learns about herself by listening to her mother and grandmother. Our favorite part of *How to Make an American Quilt* is when Finn looks on as her grandmother and great-aunt smoke pot. If this wasn't enough, she finds out that Granny slept with

Auntie's husband! Despite this conflict, Finn sees how their love endured and realizes that friendship and family outlast passion.

 Hunk Factor: 6

Finn succumbs to the handsome strawberry farmer (Johnathon Schaech), and really, who can blame her? We are soft on Dermot Mulroney, too, even when he's playing a dork.

 Hankie Factor: 5

Constance (Kate Nelligan) breaks down over losing her husband while Patsy Cline sings "You Belong to Me."

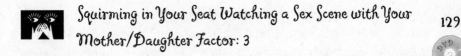 Squirming in Your Seat Watching a Sex Scene with Your Mother/Daughter Factor: 3

129

There are a few sexual moments here, some nudity, but nothing too steamy.

BEHIND THE SCENES

The Australian director Jocelyn Moorhouse produced *Muriel's Wedding*. Though poet Maya Angelou had appeared on Broadway and television, this was her first acting role in a movie.

AFTERMATH

Winona Ryder and Dermot Mulroney were nominated in the 1996 MTV Movie Awards for the best kiss.

The Joy Luck Club (1993)

Rated R

Directed by Wayne Wang

Starring Kieu Chinh, Tsai Chin, France Nuyen, Lisa Lu, Ming-Na Wen, Tamlyn Tomita, Lauren Tom, Rosalind Chao

THE PLOT

The movie interweaves the stories of four mothers, four daughters, and two cultures, feudal China and modern-day San Francisco. Stories abound (and therefore flashbacks do, too) at the weekly mahjongg game played by the mothers, Suyuan (Kieu Chinh), Lindo (Tsai Chin), An-Mei (Lisa Lu), and Ying-Ying (France Nuyen). The women suffered horribly in China: Suyuan had to leave behind her twin daughters; Lindo was married to a tubby 10-year-old; An-Mei's mother was a concubine; and Ying-Ying was a battered wife. Their American daughters struggle, too, in a less dramatic but nonetheless painful way: Jing-Mei, or June (Ming-Na Wen), the narrator, feels she can never meet her mother's expectations; Rose (Rosalind Chao) is losing her husband to another woman; Waverly (Tamlyn Tomita) is a former child prodigy who has grown into an arrogant and devious adult; and Lena (Lauren Tom) is married to a cheapskate.

The Joy Luck Club starts with the mothers and daughters, but grandparents, husbands, friends, and children round out this multi-generational story. While the movie may sound confusing, it seamlessly moves from character to character, story to story, China to the United States, and past to present.

130

❤❤ Bonding Potential: 10

You don't have to be Chinese to identify with Waverly's speech to her mom: "You don't know the power you have over me! One word from you, one look, and I'm four years old again. . . . Nothing I do can ever, ever please you." The other daughters similarly find their Old World mothers demanding, critical, and weirdly superstitious. In the course of the narrative, these young women understand the terrible price their mothers paid to escape their past. The most poignant mother-daughter story belongs to Ying-Ying and her daughter Lena. After a childhood spent trying to cope with her mother's depression, Lena finally learns her mother's tragedy: Ying-Ying was married to an abusive creep in China (too bad he's the best-looking guy in the movie) and was forced to commit a desperate act to free herself. Lena herself marries a stinker of a different ilk—her husband is so stingy that he deducts her tampons from the household budget. And he's rich, too! Learning about her mother's tragic past empowers Lena. She, like the other daughters, begins to appreciate the legacy of hope and survival that their mothers have given them.

 ## Hunk Factor: 3

The lousy bum who marries Ying-Ying is really handsome. Rose's husband, Andrew (*Breakfast Club*) McCarthy, is merely cute.

 ## Hankie Factor: 10

There are at least six separate hankie moments.

Squirming in Your Seat Watching a Sex Scene with Your Mother/Daughter Factor: 2

Why this movie got an R rating while *Heartbreakers* got a PG-13 and *Terms of Endearment* got a PG is one of those Hollywood mysteries like how Tara Reid continues to be hired.

BEHIND THE SCENES

The author of the book, Amy Tam, was born in California in 1952, the daughter of Chinese immigrants. When her mother came to the United States in 1949, she (like Suyuan) was forced to leave behind her young daughters.

AFTERMATH

Oddly, one of the movie's producers is Oliver Stone, who's hardly known for his propensity to create chick flicks.

Moonstruck (1987)

Rated PG

132

Directed by Norman Jewison

Starring Cher, Nicolas Cage, Olympia Dukakis, Vincent Gardenia, John Mahoney, Anita Gillette, Feodor Chaliapin, Danny Aiello

THE PLOT

Loretta Castorini (Cher) is a frumpy 37-year-old Italian-American woman who was widowed, a tragedy she attributes to her bad luck. She lives in a big Brooklyn brownstone with her parents, Cosmo and Rose (Vincent Gardenia and Olympia Dukakis), grandfather (Feodor Chaliapin), and a virtual kennel of dogs. The family is close and loving even though Loretta's mother suspects, correctly, that Dad is having an affair with a local floozy (Anita Gillette). Loretta decides to settle for a safe, comfortable life by accepting the marriage proposal of mama's boy Johnny Cammareri (Danny Aiello). At her fiancé's request, she seeks out his estranged brother Ronnie (Nicolas Cage) to invite him to the wedding. Loretta finds Ronnie to be angry and bitter, blaming Johnny for the loss of his hand. Somehow she finds this to be a turn-on, since within a few hours of meeting, Ronnie and Loretta become besotted with each other and fall into bed. The morning after, Loretta is overcome with guilt, and Ronnie promises to stay out of her life on the condition that she go to the opera with him that evening. She does go, but not before something of a makeover, which leaves her resembling a certain gay icon with only one name. A big December moon—*la bella luna*—shines down on their enchanted evening.

You will have to get past some hammy acting and lots of bad dye jobs, but it will be worth it: Cher and Nicolas Cage are soooooo good together. Their story is both romantic and believable. The critic who described *Moonstruck* as "a great big beautiful valentine of a movie" was right.

 Bonding Potential: 10

Loretta and her mother are both weary of life and men. The scene of them together in church beautifully depicts how close they are; it's Mom who imbues Loretta with strength and a loving nature. She inherits her honesty from Mom as well:

Cosmo: I don't like him.
Rose: You're not going to marry him, Cosmo. Do you love him, Loretta?
Loretta: No.
Rose: Good.
[Rose looks at her husband.]
Rose: When you love them they drive you crazy because they know they can.

More than anything else, *Moonstruck* is a celebration of the extended family; the film is overpopulated with mothers, fathers, sons, daughters, brothers, aunts, uncles, even an ancient grandfather. The tight-knit Italian-American families depicted here are what give the film's characters their strength. When Loretta has her final confrontation with fiancé Johnny, he wants them to talk privately. Her answer is firm: "No, I need my family around me now." Even the final words of the movie are a life- and family-affirming toast: *"A la famiglia!"*

133

Hunk Factor: 8

Nic Cage is definitely not for everyone. But we love him, especially here.

Hankie Factor: 7

Only because of the many and beautiful shots of the World Trade Center.

Squirming in Your Seat Watching a Sex Scene with Your Mother/Daughter Factor: 1

The scene when Ronnie literally and figuratively sweeps Loretta off her feet isn't really squirmable, just passionate.

134

BEHIND THE SCENES

Cher threatened to pull out of the project unless Nicolas Cage was cast as her lover Ronnie. In real life, Cage is 18 years younger than Cher. During the making of *Moonstruck,* Cher was dating Rob Camilletti, also 18 years younger. What a dame!

AFTERMATH

MGM had little faith that *Moonstruck* would be a success. It was only when their simultaneously released *Overboard* tanked that the studio decided to put its publicity efforts behind it. Cher, Olympia Dukakis, and writer John Patrick Shanley all won Academy Awards.

My Life as a Dog (1985)

Not rated

Directed by Lasse Hallström

Starring Anton Glanzelius, Tomas von Brömssen, Anki Liden, Melinda Kinnaman, Kicki Rundgren, Ing-mari Carlsson

THE PLOT

Ingemar (Anton Glanzelius) is a precocious 12-year-old who just can't seem to keep out of mischief. He proves to be too much for his terminally ill mother (Anki Liden), so he's forced to leave his beloved dog Sickan to live in the country with his uncle Gunnar (Tomas von Brömssen) and aunt Ulla (Kicki Rundgren). Ingemar fits in with his uncle's village of eccentrics, making friends and joining the soccer team, where he meets Saga (Melinda Kinnaman), a girl pretending to be a boy so she can remain in the league. Ingemar and Saga become partners in both sport and in sexual awakening. After his mother's death, Ingemar tries to cope with loss, guilt, and two girls vying for his affection. Ingemar's solution? He makes believe he's a dog.

Okay, so the main character is a son, not a daughter. This is still one of the greatest coming-of-age movies ever. It's funny, tragic, hopeful, and so natural that you forget that everyone is talking in Swedish. The tiny village embraces the motherless boy, becoming a makeshift family of tightrope walkers, nude models, glassblowers, and even the old man who's fixated on a lingerie catalogue.

Bonding Potential: 8

Moms, daughters—in fact, anyone who's ever been a child—can relate to Ingemar, whose pain and joy are so vivid and palpable. Ingemar tries to hold on to his sick mother, make her well, make her laugh, but usually he winds up driving her crazy. The scene where his mother completely loses it will resonate with any mother who feels like she just can't take it anymore. Ingemar makes a case that kids are sometimes treated like dogs and compares himself to Laika, the dog the Russians sent into space, only to forget the Puppy Chow. More than anything else, *My Life as a Dog* is about the courage and resilience of children.

Hunk Factor: 0

Hankie Factor: 8

His mom is dying. And the dog has seen better days, too.

Squirming in Your Seat Watching a Sex Scene with Your Mother/Daughter Factor: 1

Some nudity and preadolescent experimentation.

BEHIND THE SCENES

My Life as a Dog is based on the autobiographical novel of Reidar Jönssen, who as an adolescent lived alone in an apartment for a year after his mother's death.

AFTERMATH

The international success of this movie made its director, Lasse Hallström, famous. He went on to direct several Hollywood movies, including *What's Eating Gilbert Grape?* and *Chocolat.*

Parenthood (1989)

Rated PG-13

Directed by Ron Howard

Starring Steve Martin, Dianne Wiest, Dennis Dugan, Mary Steenburgen, Jason Robards Jr., Rick Moranis, Tom Hulce, Martha Plimpton, Keanu Reeves, Harley Jane Kozak, Joaquin Phoenix

THE PLOT

Parenthood is a comedy about modern life and the never-ending responsibilities of raising children. Gil Buckman (Steve Martin), the husband of Karen (Mary Steenburgen) and father to three children, tries to find a balance between family and career. He puts his family first and is determined to be more involved than his own father (Jason Robards Jr.) was with him. His three siblings round out Gil's family. His sister, Helen Buckman Lampkin Bowman (Dianne Wiest), is a lonely and divorced mother of two unruly children she doesn't understand (Martha Plimpton and Joaquin Phoenix). Gil's brother, Larry Buckman (Tom Hulce), is the black sheep of the family who shows up at his aging parents' house with a biracial child named Cool, looking to scam some cash. Their kid sister, Susan (Harley Jane Kozak), is married to Nathan (Rick Moranis), a father so obsessed with having an intellectually precocious child that he reads Kafka to his 3-year-old.

This movie takes on the sensitive subject of a child with needs. Gil and Karen have a child with emotional problems who may need to go to a special school. This embarrasses Gil, and he blames himself for not being the perfect dad. But when the kid finally triumphs on the Little League field, Gil rejoices with pure unadulterated joy.

137

Bonding Potential: 8

Because it is a multigenerational story (four are represented here), nearly everyone is able to see themselves as a parent and as a child.

As parents, they are all responding to the way they were treated as children.

 Hunk Factor: 4

Hunky is a stretch, but Keanu Reeves is young, earnest, and cute.

 Hankie Factor: 0

All laughs, no tears.

 Squirming in Your Seat Watching a Sex Scene with Your Mother/Daughter Factor: 7

There are some sexual situations in the movie, but the squirmiest moments are when a vibrator shows up—twice.

BEHIND THE SCENES

Director Ron Howard has four children, Mary Steenburgen has two, Rick Moranis has two, and Jason Robards Jr. had nine. However, Steve Martin, who put the *parent* in *Parenthood*, has never been a father.

AFTERMATH

Dianne Wiest was nominated for an Oscar and a Golden Globe as best supporting actress.

William Shakespeare's Romeo & Juliet (1996)
Rated PG-13

Directed by Baz Luhrmann
Starring Claire Danes, Leonardo DiCaprio, Brian Dennehy, John Leguizamo, Paul
Sorvino

THE PLOT

We lay our scene in fair Verona, now a shamble of broken down
beachside carnivals and imposing smog-incrusted skyscrapers,
where two households, gangs really, both alike in dignity, wage a
bloody war in the streets and on the evening news. Baz Luhrmann's
Romeo & Juliet is definitely not for everybody. Shakespeare's enduring tragedy is not only updated to the modern day but crazily adrena-
lized, and though many of the Bard's best lines are lost amid music
video montages or simply mangled in the mouths of earnest but un-
trained actors, the movie is a fever dream of young love. There may
be productions of *Romeo & Juliet* more competently or elegantly done,
but none so passionately felt.

139

To recap: Star-crossed lovers from feuding families meet, marry,
and end badly. This time around, expect Hawaiian shirts and hand-
guns instead of doublets and rapiers; expect Radiohead and Prince
on the soundtrack instead of mandolins. Baz Luhrmann, director of
the similarly much loved or much despised *Moulin Rouge*, stages a
visionary and heartbreaking pageant of love found and lost, but the
film's editing and camera work are so relentless and dizzying that you
may feel as though you're stuck in the middle of some Mardi Gras parade. As the ill-fated pair, Leonardo DiCaprio and Claire Danes are
both exceedingly young and perfectly cast. DiCaprio isn't so good with
iambic pentameter—he speaks some soliloquies as if he's squeaking
out the instructions to his VCR—but his Romeo is marvelously fluid:
by turns brooding and goofy, ecstatic and furious. Danes, however, is
the more commanding presence; her Juliet strikes a balance between
delicate and powerful, innocent and sexual.

Bonding Potential: 7

For a young person, Shakespeare's plays call to mind many things—Spark Notes, hammy actors trotting out their best Elizabethan accents, ill-fitting tights—but rarely is a futuristic thrill ride among them. Mothers will most likely marvel at this bold and clever take on an old favorite, and daughters will appreciate its resemblance to MTV, only with substance and heart. *Romeo & Juliet,* fast-paced and emotionally raw, is certainly more accessible to young people than a more traditional production. And viewers young and old will respond to the love scenes between DiCaprio and Danes, which take on a timelessness that transcends both Luhrmann's hyperstylized direction and Shakespeare's familiar prose.

 Hunk Factor: 7

Romeo & Juliet delivers a DiCaprio from the days when he was the Indie answer to Freddie Prinze Jr., all lanky limbs and filled with promise, before his mystique and quirkiness were forever submerged in the Atlantic's icy waters along with a certain ill-fated cruise liner.

 Hankie Factor: 8

Romeo & Juliet is the prototype tearjerker, and it has more broken hearts under its belt than any other tragedy. In this, if with nothing else, Luhrmann's version holds with tradition.

Squirming in Your Seat Watching a Sex Scene with Your Mother/Daughter Factor: 0

The love scenes here are sweet and chaste (as opposed to the rest of the movie), even more so than the Franco Zeffirelli version from

1968, which famously showed the teenage lovers naked in bed the morning after their honeymoon night.

BEHIND THE SCENES

Luhrmann went to great lengths to create a modern Verona Beach worthy of the Bard. The cityscape is littered with references to his other works like some kind of Shakespearean product placement. Pay close attention to the preponderance of neon signs and advertisements scattered throughout the film and you will notice that they are filled with Shakespearean in-jokes. For example, "Experience is by industry achieved" (in the Capulet lift) is from *The Two Gentlemen of Verona*, act I, scene III, line 25. "Such stuff as dreams are made on" (another ad) is from *The Tempest,* act IV, scene I, lines 168–169. Prospero (the name of the drink in the ad) is the player who says these lines.

AFTERMATH

141

Luhrmann's follow-up film, *Moulin Rouge,* was a commercial and critical success. DiCaprio, as even children in the African bush know, went on to Big Things, and Danes not only studied at Yale but appeared in *Terminator 3: Rise of the Machines.*

The Secret Life of Girls (1998)
Rated PG

Directed by Holly Goldberg Sloan
Starring Linda Hamilton, Eugene Levy, Majandra Defino, Meagan Good, Aeryk Egan, Andrew Ducote

THE PLOT

Fifteen-year-old Natalie (Majandra Defino) is a bookish middle child in a family of eccentrics. Her father Hugh (Eugene Levy) is a psychology professor who has difficulty communicating, and her mother Ruby (Linda Hamilton) is a quirky collector of architectural elements (like staircases). Natalie has a pothead older brother, Jim (Aeryk Egan), and a younger brother, Andy (Andrew Ducote), who wears a

DADDY'S LITTLE GIRL

I'm a father. Worry comes with the territory.
—STEVE MARTIN, *Father of the Bride*

1. *To Kill a Mockingbird*

2. *Man on the Moon*

3. *Matchstick Men*

4. *Meet the Parents*

5. *Father of the Bride*

6. *Guess Who's Coming to Dinner*

7. *Prizzi's Honor*

8. *Sorry, Wrong Number*

9. *Three Men and a Baby*

10. *I Am Sam*

11. *The Golden Bowl*

12. *Paper Moon*

13. *Magnolia*

14. *On Golden Pond*

15. *The Heiress*

different hat every day. She finds refuge in friend Kay (Meagan Good), and the two are the quintessential teenage best friends. When the family discovers that Hugh has had an affair with one of his students, Ruby leads Natalie and Kay on a mission for the truth.

The story follows the twists and turns of the disintegrating family unit, and leads nearly everyone to a better understanding of themselves and the world. In the idyllic closing scene of the movie, after the fury of the divorce has waned, Natalie and Kay go for a carefree swim in the lake. Natalie reflects, "I guess the most important thing you can do for a kid is show them how to be a good parent when they grow up. If you can do that, then you've done your job. So how do you teach them, by doing it right or by doing it wrong? Or in the end is there no right or wrong as long as they know that you love them."

 Bonding Potential: 7

This is about a family that deteriorates, then rebuilds within a new structure, and in the process everyone's relationships are redefined. This brings up a lot of stuff to talk about. Working moms will feel encouraged when Natalie says, "Everyone in the neighborhood had stay-at-home moms. Maybe that's why everyone started drinking at six."

143

 Hunk Factor: 0

Hankie Factor: 0

Squirming in Your Seat Watching a Sex Scene with Your Mother/Daughter Factor: 3

There are no sex scenes in this movie, but there is a difficult scene where a college dropout preys on the naive young Natalie after feeding her Jell-O shots. It is enough to cause anyone to squirm.

BEHIND THE SCENES

This is an autobiographical story of the director, Holly Goldberg Sloan. Her real family reunited for the last scene and is mixed in with the actors. The movie was originally called *American Pie,* but the other *American Pie* beat them to the theaters. Coincidentally, Eugene Levy was in both films.

Spellbound (2003)
Rated G

Directed by Jeffrey Blitz
Starring Harry Altman, Angela Arenivar, Ted Brigham, April DeGideo, Neil Kadakia,
Nupur Lala, Emily Stagg, Ashley White

144

THE PLOT

A documentary about the 1999 National Spelling Bee, *Spellbound* follows eight contestants—mostly seventh and eighth graders—from their hometowns to the national contest in Washington, D.C. The filmmakers go inside the contestants' homes and lives. They let the kids and their families just talk, a very effective way to show how different their backgrounds are. By the time *Spellbound* gets to the final contest in Washington, we know and care about each of the eight contestants. One thing they all have in common, besides braces, is that they are outsiders in their world. Their parents support them—some even live through them—but don't really understand them. *Spellbound* shows that small-town Americana survives: Local businesses, even Hooters, offer words of encouragement—often misspelled—to the contestants as they head off to Washington. *It's a Wonderful Life* meets *Revenge of the Nerds.*

This may be hard to believe, but this documentary about spelling has suspense, emotion, and lots of heart. We got so involved with this movie that, we have to confess, we had our two favorites among the contestants. Of course we won't tell you who they were, but let's just say they were girls. We also had our least favorite. Ritalin, anyone?

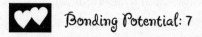 **Bonding Potential: 7**

Spelling bees are, in a word, old-fashioned. Daughters, who grew up with spell-check, share this experience with their mothers, grand-mothers, and great-grandmothers. All generations can remember cursing the perversity of the English language while waiting their turn to spell a word. If your daughter accuses you of being too strict about studying and schoolwork, tell her to check out Neil's dad. He asks his son to spell 7,000 to 8,000 words a day and uses a micro-phone to quiz him—while they're sitting two feet apart. FYI: The win-ning word was *logorrhea,* which isn't a malady caused by bad shellfish, but rather excessive talkativeness.

145

 Hunk Factor: 0

What did you expect? This is a documentary with real people, not actors.

 Hankie Factor: 2

Our fave didn't win.

 Squirming in Your Seat Watching a Sex Scene with Your Mother/Daughter Factor: 0

BEHIND THE SCENES

Spellbound director Jeffrey Blitz said he financed almost all of it on credit cards.

AFTERMATH

The movie was nominated for an Oscar, which meant that Blitz got to go onstage when Michael Moore invited all of the nominees to be part of the controversial speech he made when accepting for *Bowling for Columbine.*

Terms of Endearment (1983)
Rated PG

Directed by James L. Brooks

Starring Shirley MacLaine, Debra Winger, Jack Nicholson, John Lithgow, Jeff Daniels

THE PLOT

146

Widowed Aurora Greenway (Shirley MacLaine) lives in an upper-class suburb of Houston with her only child, Emma (Debra Winger). Aurora, who is simultaneously overprotective of *and* insulting to her daughter, surrounds herself with male admirers. Emma, in turn, rushes into an early marriage with a graduate student, the unreliable Flap (Jeff Daniels). Despite their incessant fighting, Emma and Aurora are close and manage to remain so, even after Emma moves to Iowa. She and Flap proceed to have three children, and the family is living only slightly above the poverty line when Emma discovers Flap, now a junior professor, has been unfaithful. She manages to find some solace in a brief romance with a timid banker, Sam (John Lithgow). Back in Houston, Aurora begins an affair with her neighbor, astronaut-turned-skirtchaser-turned-souse Garrett Breedlove (Jack Nicholson). Then *Terms of Endearment,* which started out as a comedy about mothers, daughters, middle-aged sex, and wig extensions, takes a sudden, heartbreaking turn.

What a reassuring message Aurora and Emma give us. No matter how much or how often you fight, mothers and daughters can be intimate and loving. These characters are pretty honest with each other, too. Besides dishing about their respective love lives, they speak to each other so bluntly that at times it seems almost shocking. On the night before Emma's marriage, Aurora flatly informs her, "You are not special enough to overcome a bad marriage."

 Bonding Potential: 10

Emma is one of those daughters—there are lots of you out there, admit it—who make a point of being as different from their mothers as possible. She dresses plainly, eschews makeup, and wears socks with her (flannel) nightgown. Aurora, on the other hand, dresses as though she raided Blanche DuBois's closet, wears two coats of Great Lash, and clip-clops through Houston in impossibly high heels. In one of the many great scenes in *Terms of Endearment,* Aurora, having presumably left her makeup at home, is plain and ravaged. She is a lioness who fights the hospital staff to get her daughter pain medication, screaming, "My daughter is in pain, can't you understand that! *Give my daughter the shot!*"

147

 Hunk Factor: 5

Applicable to Nicholson fans only.

 Hankie Factor: 10

You'll laugh, you'll cry.

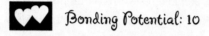 **Squirming in Your Seat Watching a Sex Scene with Your Mother/Daughter Factor: 0**

BEHIND THE SCENES

As close as they were as a mother and daughter in the movies, that's how much MacLaine and Winger hated each other in real life. Each refused to speak to the other in between scenes, and at one point they even got into a shoving match. Ladies, please! In her autobiography, *My Lucky Stars,* MacLaine said that on their second meeting, Winger "looked over her shoulder, bent over and farted in my face." Still, Winger managed to find the time to start her romance with the then governor of Nebraska, Bob Kerrey.

AFTERMATH

This movie swept the Oscars, winning awards for Nicholson, MacLaine, and director Brooks as well as best picture of the year.

148

Dirty Dancing (1987)
Rated PG-13

Directed by Emile Ardolino
Starring Jennifer Grey, Patrick Swayze, Jerry Orbach, Cynthia Rhodes, Jack Weston,
Kelly Bishop

THE PLOT

Our video store's worn-out tape of *Dirty Dancing* has probably been in the VCRs of an incalculable number of women whose nights began with home facials and ended with heaping spoonfuls of raw cookie dough. It's still the guiltiest guilty pleasure for a generation of girls who hope that if a merengue-ing, leather-jacket-wearing tough guy isn't about to sweep them off their feet, then at the very least their boyfriends might finally be coaxed into a couple of turns on the dance floor. For readers who have spent their entire lives at the North Pole (although, come to think of it, we'd bet that more than a few young

MAMA'S BOYS

A boy's best friend is his mother.
—ANTHONY PERKINS, *Psycho*

1. *Mother*

2. *Flirting with Disaster*

3. *White Heat*

4. *Murmur of the Heart*

5. *Chafed Elbows*

6. *The Manchurian Candidate*

7. *Marty*

8. *Affair of the Heart*

9. *Monster's Ball*

10. *The Deep End*

11. *Ordinary People*

12. *In the Bedroom*

13. *The Sixth Sense*

14. *The Graduate*

15. *Throw Momma from the Train*

149

girls there have hooked the generator up to the igloo in order to watch Patrick Swayze's butt), *Dirty Dancing* stars a pre-nose-job Jennifer Grey as Baby, a 17-year-old on vacation in the Catskills with her well-to-do parents (Jerry Orbach and Kelly Bishop) in the summer of 1963. Swayze plays Johnny, the hotel dance instructor—he's Gene Kelly from the waist down and Brando from the waist up—and as when any two people from different worlds meet in the movies, he and Baby wind up first as dance partners and then as lovers. There's not a ton of plot, but the dancing really is pretty thrilling, and Grey and Swayze do more with their hips and eyes than most actors can do with a hundred lines of dialogue. By the time Swayze declares, "Nobody puts Baby in the corner," you'll be ready to hop up and mambo in your pajamas.

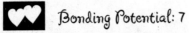 Bonding Potential: 7

You don't exactly watch *Dirty Dancing* for the sensitive rendering of a tightly knit mother-daughter team. In fact, Baby's mother hardly has a role to speak of, except to pipe in at the end in defense of Baby's cavorting with Johnny. It seems that lusting after the hot hoofer runs in the family. Even though Baby and her mother don't have much rapport, *Dirty Dancing* has plenty of bonding potential. Sure, Baby's annoyingly and vociferously idealistic, but her evolution into a self-possessed young woman is nevertheless touching. *Dirty Dancing* is a romantic coming-of-age flick with great dance sequences that can also serve as an introduction to more serious topics, such as first sexual experiences, class and gender, and the history of women's reproductive rights.

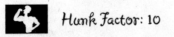 Hunk Factor: 10

Patrick Swayze's got moves. Nuff said.

Hankie Factor: 4

As Baby pursues Johnny, her status as Daddy's little princess is compromised, and it's moving to watch her and her father try to grow into the next stage of their relationship.

 Squirming in Your Seat Watching a Sex Scene with Your Mother/Daughter Factor: 8

Mothers should be forewarned that there is action off of the dance floor, too. In addition to some minor nudity and sexual content, there is a subplot involving an illegal abortion gone wrong.

BEHIND THE SCENES

Patrick Swayze provided the vocals on the film's signature song "She's Like the Wind."

AFTERMATH

Swayze went on to win the further affections of women everywhere by starring in *Ghost* and *Point Break,* but has since fallen from grace as a premier hunk. He will be reprising his role as Johnny in the *forthcoming* sequel *Dirty Dancing: Havana Nights*, so perhaps a Swayze renaissance is imminent.

Jennifer Grey had a nose job that left us all wondering if she'd gone into the federal witness protection program. In order to confirm that in fact this newly button-nosed beauty was in fact still the girl from *Dirty Dancing*, she played herself on the short-lived 1999 sitcom *It's Like, You Know* . . .

The mother, Kelly Bishop (who also won a Tony as Sheila in the original production of *A Chorus Line*), went on to play Lorelei's perfectionist mother in the TV series *The Gilmore Girls*.

In 1997, Conan O'Brien jokingly started a petition to get *Dirty Dancing* re-released for its tenth anniversary. When he realized with horror that the movement was gaining steam, he spent his time on air deriding *Dirty Dancing*.

OLDER TEENS ONLY

The Royal Tenenbaums (2001)

Rated R

Directed by Wes Anderson
Starring Gene Hackman, Anjelica Huston, Gwyneth Paltrow, Luke Wilson, Owen
Wilson, Danny Glover, Ben Stiller, Bill Murray

THE PLOT

In a fairy-tale New York at once grand and dilapidated, a family of has-been child prodigies has grown into adults ruined by "two decades of failure, betrayal and disaster." They are a strange, sad bunch, each uniquely gifted, each unbearably troubled: Margot (Gwyneth Paltrow), a playwright who hasn't written a word in years; Richie (Luke Wilson), a disgraced tennis champ, stricken with love for his adopted sister; and Chas (Ben Stiller), a financial whiz and almost psychotically protective father, grieving furiously over the death of his wife. The film's ostensible plot is set in motion when their father, Royal (Gene Hackman), a disreputable lawyer who abandoned them long ago, conspires to win back his family.

The Tenenbaum house, this ramshackle brownstone of empty ballrooms and tiny closets crammed with beautiful junk, is crowded with folks as colorful as cartoons. There's the Tenenbaum matriarch, Etheline (Anjelica Huston), who plays nurse to these asylum inmates. There are Chas's two kids, Uzi and Ari, each in identical bright red sweat suits. There's Raleigh (Bill Murray), Margot's gentle anthropologist husband; Eli Cash (Owen Wilson), their childhood next-door neighbor who's grown up to be a drug-addled writer of westerns; Henry Sherman (Danny Glover), Etheline's accountant and fiancé; not to mention Pagoda (Kumar Pallana), the family butler (who first met Royal when he was hired to kill him in Calcutta).

152

Hackman's performance here should have won him an Oscar. As scandalous, selfish, rambunctious Royal, he first cons his kids into loving him and then finally falls in love with them. The movie itself is a marvelous achievement, dense with sadness and humor.

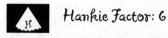 ## Bonding Potential: 6

The Royal Tenenbaums is a movie about a family that is wrecked and then rebuilt. Mom's the only real grown-up, extremely caring, but while she is inoculated against the many eccentricities of her children, she seems slightly unresponsive to their troubles (one might say that their eccentricities are their troubles, and so by accepting one, she ignores the other). No, it'll take Royal—who originally shows up just looking for a handout, who doesn't want Etheline back so much as he doesn't want her with anyone else—to help heal their family. The movie, then, is the education of Royal Tenenbaum, as this dissolute, self-interested, often insincere man learns to become a loving father to his now grown children. His long absence is what afflicts each of them (though his infrequent presence when they were kids was hardly better), and when he gives them reason to forgive him, they are finally freed from their arrested, now curdled childhoods to be actual functioning adults. At the beginning, the Tenenbaums make Oedipus's family look close, but by its end, this movie offers us a vision of family as the best way of saving us from ourselves.

Hunk Factor: 4

The Wilson brothers are considered hunks. So, for some reason, is Ben Stiller.

Hankie Factor: 6

A suicide attempt by one of the characters, set to Elliot Smith's "Needle in the Hay," is wrenching, as the screen floods with memories and then with blood. And the reconciliation between Royal and angry, bitter Chas is completed with a single simple line, heartbreakingly delivered.

 Squirming in Your Seat Watching a Sex Scene with Your Mother/Daughter Factor: 0

BEHIND THE SCENES

Director Wes Anderson and writer/actor Owen Wilson were college pals who collaborated on *Rushmore* and *Bottle Rocket* before this movie. Anderson based the character of Etheline on his mother, and Anjelica Huston even wears his mother's glasses throughout the film. On the romance front, Luke Wilson and Gwyneth Paltrow made good on their characters' semi-incestuous impulses by becoming romantically involved during shooting.

154

AFTERMATH

Alas, Luke and Gwyneth broke up. But in true Tenenbaum spirit, Luke and Owen Wilson are roommates.

Two Women (La Ciociara) (1960)

Not rated

Directed by Vittorio De Sica
Starring Sophia Loren, Raf Vallone, Jean-Paul Belmondo, Eleanora Brown

THE PLOT

Cesira (Sophia Loren) and her 13-year-old daughter, Rosetta (Eleanora Brown), struggle to survive in Italy at the end of World War II. Cesira, in an effort to protect her daughter from the constant bombing, leaves

Rome and her married boyfriend (Raf Vallone) to return to her native village. There she meets Michele (Jean-Paul Belmondo), an antifascist. After Mussolini is killed, mother and daughter head back to Rome; on the way, they are raped by allied Moroccan soldiers in a bombed-out church.

A word to the wise: The quality of the VHS and DVD could be better. It's a lucky thing this is such a great movie, or else folks might have a hard time dealing with the washed-out picture and tinny sound.

Bonding Potential: 10

It's a fact: As much as a mother will try, she can't shelter her kids from the trials of life, especially if there's a war going on. No movie illustrates this more than *Two Women*. Cesira fights to keep Rosetta safe from bombs, hunger, flirty fascists, nosy neighbors, and lecherous teenage boys. All her efforts suddenly, tragically fail.

Hunk Factor: 7

155

Our rating can be summed up in three words: Belmondo, Belmondo, Belmondo. He makes the foreign exchange student inside us squeal with pleasure.

Hankie Factor: 10

This is one of the most powerful antiwar movies ever made because you live the war through just two characters, the mother and daughter. One of the most poignant scenes in the movie is a mother gone mad who offers her breast milk to Cesira since her own child has died.

 ### Squirming in Your Seat Watching a Sex Scene with Your Mother/Daughter Factor: 4

The rape scene is difficult for anybody to watch.

BEHIND THE SCENES

Sophia Loren drew on the poverty of her own war-torn childhood in Rome for *Two Women*. Her mother, like Cesira, was single. Two years after this movie was made, Sophia's marriage to the film's producer, Carlo Ponti, was annulled; the Italian court claimed Ponti was a bigamist. They weren't able to be legally married until years later.

AFTERMATH

When Sophia Loren deservedly won an Oscar for *Two Women*, she was the first actor in a foreign film to be bestowed with this honor. She wanted to prove to the world that she was not just another "sexy pot." Not bad for someone who got her start in Italian skin flicks! Still acting from time to time, Sophia also writes cookbooks and promotes eyewear (i.e., glasses) that look horrible on anyone *but* Sophia Loren.

A Walk on the Moon (1999)
Rated R

Directed by Tony Goldwyn
Starring Diane Lane, Liev Schreiber, Anna Paquin, Viggo Mortensen, Tovah Feldshuh

THE PLOT

Pearl Kantrowitz (Diane Lane) is a young housewife vacationing in a bungalow community in the Catskills while hubby Marty (Liev Schreiber) spends weekdays in the city. It is the summer of 1969, and Pearl is questioning her place in a changing world. When she meets a hippie hunk named Walker Jerome (Viggo Mortensen), he opens Pearl's eyes. In the meantime, her daughter Alison (Anna Paquin) is brimming with adolescent angst and nosy mother-in-law (Tovah Feldshuh) is snooping around the whole mess. Pearl and Alison, each unbeknownst to the other, sneak out to go to the Woodstock Festival.

Marty's mother calls and tells him to hustle up to the Catskills, and fast.

This is the story of a woman thrown into a sexistential crisis. Pearl, a teenage bride, is reaching for the lost years of her youth just as her daughter is moving toward womanhood. The walk on the moon in the title refers to Neil Armstrong's lunar landing and mother and daughter's first step into a new world.

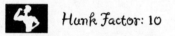 Bonding Potential: 8

There is a memorable scene when Alison confronts Pearl about her affair. It's honest and painful and could open a discussion of difficult issues. *A Walk on the Moon* also has a touching scene when Alison gets her first period. We see three generations of women react to this female rite of passage, which includes the familiar line "Don't tell Daddy I got my period."

 Hunk Factor: 10

It's really hard to get any hunkier than Viggo Mortensen.

 Hankie Factor: 7

Bring 'em on for the final scene of Pearl and Walker in his garden.

Squirming in Your Seat Watching a Sex Scene with Your Mother/Daughter Factor: 9

This is definitely not for younger girls: The love scenes between Pearl and Walker in the back of the bus and under a waterfall are among the best ever and earned this movie its R rating.

BEHIND THE SCENES

Liev Schreiber plays the anti-Woodstock square in this movie, but in
real life, his parents were hippies who moved to Canada to set up a
health food store during the Vietnam years. When Diane Lane talked
about Pearl, she defended her character's affair by saying that Pearl
never had her teenage years. Neither, for that matter, did Diane: She
was a child star and on the cover of *Time* magazine at the age of 13.

AFTERMATH

Diane Lane's sensitive, sympathetic performance as an adulteress no
doubt led to her role as another sensitive, sympathetic adulteress in
2002's *Unfaithful*.

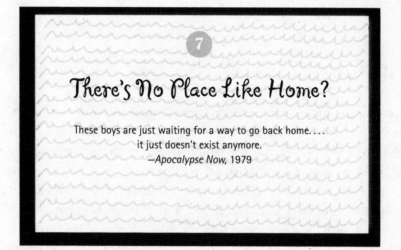

Business executives on scooters? Grandma in hot pants? Folks these days don't seem to want to grow up. Try as we might, we can't stay children forever, and until the advent of the time travel machine, we really can't go home again. In this chapter, we highlight some of the most shameless attempts at regression this side of never-never land.

An American Rhapsody (2001)

Rated PG-13

Directed by Éva Gárdos

Starring Natassja Kinski, Tony Goldwyn, Scarlett Johansson, Mae Whitman, Agi
    Bánfalvy

THE PLOT

The movie opens with Suzanne's (Scarlett Johansson) voiceover: "I was 15 and my life was already falling apart, so I came back to Hungary where it all began." We soon learn that when Suzanne was an infant, her mother Margit (Natassja Kinski), father Peter (Tony Goldwyn), and older sister (Mae Whitman) escaped from Hungary, but were forced to leave her behind. Her grandmother (Agi Bánfalvy) left her with foster parents, who lovingly raised her as their own in the Hungarian countryside. At 6, Suzanne is reunited with her parents and sister in Southern California. She adjusts to American life, but understandably develops some emotional problems as a teenager. She feels that she is caught between two worlds and must return to Hungary to understand her identity and herself.

In this true story of her background, writer-director Éva Gárdos generously focuses much of the story on her mother and the anguish she experienced on being separated from her daughter for six years. On Suzanne's first night in the United States, her mother gets to tuck her in, kisses her, and says good night. Suzanne replies with "Good night, lady." Ouch!

♥♥ *Bonding Potential:* 10

American parents have a hard time (to put it mildly) when their teenagers start acting out. In the course of *An American Rhapsody,* Suzanne smokes, runs around with boys, and in the final coup de grâce, shoots up her room with a rifle. Imagine how difficult it is for

160

Suzanne's immigrant mother to accept this behavior; after all, she grew up under the Nazis and Stalin. So we can't fault Mom for bringing up her refugee experience: "Do you know what your father and I had to go through for you?" This mother-daughter conflict, which is both cultural as well as generational in nature, is resolved only when Suzanne returns to Hungary and learns how much her mother has endured.

 Hunk Factor: 0

 Hankie Factor: 4

Pull out the hankies for the scene when Suzanne reunites with her Hungarian foster family.

 Squirming in Your Seat Watching a Sex Scene with Your Mother/Daughter Factor: 0

No sex scenes, but some sloppy kissing.

BEHIND THE SCENES

There is a scene showing Suzanne arriving in America and the nightly news covering the story of the little girl from behind the iron curtain. The director recalled that when she saw herself on TV that night, it was the first time she had ever seen a television set.

AFTERMATH

An American Rhapsody has been confused with a book of the same name, which was written by another Hungarian-American, the screenwriter Joe Eszterhas, who brought us films like *Basic Instinct* and *Showgirls.* It's safe to assume that his book, unlike this movie, doesn't deal sweetly and generously with beautifully rendered female characters.

Coal Miner's Daughter (1980)

Rated PG

Directed by Michael Apted

Starring Sissy Spacek, Tommy Lee Jones, Levon Helm, Beverly D'Angelo, William Sanderson, Phyllis Boyens

THE PLOT

Based on her best-selling autobiography, this is Loretta Lynn's story—from an impoverished family in an Appalachian coal mining community (even village is too big a word for it) to one of the most successful and beloved country singers in the world. Loretta (Sissy Spacek) is the eldest of Clara and Ted Webb's (Phyllis Boyens and Levon Helm) many children. At 13, she marries local renegade Doolittle Lynn (Tommy Lee Jones), the man she stayed with until his death in 1996. It's not an easy marriage, but there is a lot of love and a deep connection. As Dollarhide (William Sanderson), the local moonshine distiller, tells Doolittle, "If you're born in the mountains you got three choices: coal mine, moonshine, or movin' on down the line." Doo and Loretta choose the third option and leave Butcher Hollow for greener pastures—anything would be greener than a coal mine. After hearing her sing to their ever-growing family, Doolittle decides to promote Loretta's singing career. She records a single and they do a mass mailing before driving from one radio station to the next, asking DJs to play it. On one of their stops, they learn that it is a hit. Loretta makes her debut at the Grand Ole Opry, befriends Patsy Cline (Beverly D'Angelo), and is on her way up, up, up. That is, until she hits a temporary snag.

Apted cast many local people in the Kentucky scenes. None of the ten children in the movie were actors, and only two of them went on to do one more film. This gave extra depth and insight to the early part of her life and the film. *Coal Miner's Daughter* focuses on Loretta and Doo's marriage. It's a union that endures despite the pressures of fame, separation, switched roles, drinking, and carousing in lives that take unexpected turns.

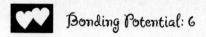 Bonding Potential: 6

Loretta Lynn's life has a message for mothers and daughters. Lynn came from a place so small that her experience was limited, yet she was thrust into an unimaginably complicated new world: touring, playing in front of huge crowds, and making friends with famous people, all while being a mother and a wife. She is challenged throughout her life—first as a teenage wife and mother and later as a woman far more successful and recognized than her husband. Her life opens up, but in a fundamental way she stays the same person: kind, loving, devoted, and straightforward.

 Hunk Factor: 6

Tommy Lee Jones is young and macho.

163

 Hankie Factor: 2

Might come in handy for some of the more emotionally intense scenes.

 Squirming in Your Seat Watching a Sex Scene with Your Mother/Daughter Factor: 0

No squirms.

BEHIND THE SCENES

When Sissy was trying to decide whether or not to make the movie, she was at the house of her mother-in-law, who said that Sissy should ask the man upstairs for a sign. Driving out of the garage, Sissy heard Loretta singing "Coal Miner's Daughter" on the radio. She turned right around and called to accept the part. Beverly D'Angelo and Sissy Spacek did all their own singing.

AFTERMATH

Sissy Spacek won an Academy Award (best actress) and Ralf Bode (cinematographer) was nominated along with John Corso and John Dwyer (art direction), Arthur Schmidt (editing), and Thomas Rickman (script). The movie was also nominated for best picture.

Far from Heaven (2002)
Rated PG-13

Directed by Todd Haynes
Starring Julianne Moore, Dennis Quaid, Dennis Haysbert, Patricia Clarkson, Ryan
  Ward, Lindsay Andretta

THE PLOT

Cathy and Frank Whitaker (Julianne Moore and Dennis Quaid) comprise a suburban, corporate couple in 1957 Connecticut with two perfect children (Ryan Ward and Lindsay Andretta). Cathy loves her life ("I've never wanted any other") until she walks in on her husband in the arms of another . . . man. Frank sees a psychiatrist to be "cured" while Cathy keeps his secret, even from her best friend, Eleanor (Patricia Clarkson). Cathy keeps her family going as well until her friendship with the gardener (Dennis Haysbert), an African-American widower, starts the town talking. Once she's seen entering a "colored" diner, Cathy becomes a social outcast. Her platonic relationship with Raymond proves to be a greater threat to her family than her husband's homosexuality.

The fifties were a repressed time for everyone, but especially for women. Before the sixties, civil rights, the women's movement, and gay rights, there was Cathy's "perfect" world of bigotry and lies. *Far from Heaven* educates us, particularly young women, about this not-so-distant past. It brings us right back to 1957: We can even smell Cathy's Aqua-Net hair spray and hear her crinolines rustle.

 Bonding Potential: 8

Early in the movie, Cathy's daughter Janice watches her brushing her hair and asks if she's going to grow up to be beautiful like her. Cathy *is* beautiful and so is her world, even as it's on the verge of falling apart. Later, when Mom is a social outcast, her daughter is, too. It's painful to see Janice shunned by everyone, even other kids, at her ballet recital. Raymond's young daughter suffers as well. And all Cathy and Raymond did was one slow dance!

 Hunk Factor: 6

Dennis Haysbert (the president on *24*) is sexy and handsome. Dennis Quaid can be appealing but not here; he looks as if he's battling Irritable Bowel syndrome.

165

Hankie Factor: 5

Raymond tells Cathy that he imagines a world where people could "see beyond the color, the surface of things." Still dry-eyed? Wait for the final scene at the train station.

Squirming in Your Seat Watching a Sex Scene with Your Mother/Daughter Factor: 0

BEHIND THE SCENES

Director Todd Haynes made this in the tradition of the great woman's films of Douglas Sirk (see *Imitation of Life*). He particularly drew from

All That Heaven Allows (1955), which starred Rock Hudson, who ironically was the most closeted actor in Hollywood history. In 1985, when Hudson revealed he had AIDS, it was a turning point for public awareness of the disease.

AFTERMATH

Julianne Moore won the Independent Spirit Award for best actress of 2002. In her acceptance speech she related a story about the director, Todd Haynes: Just as they were about to start shooting, she told him she was pregnant. His response? He told her how happy he was for her. What a guy! The actress made her pregnancy work for her—she looked like a pretty, plumpish housewife in (really) big dresses.

Rabbit-Proof Fence (2002)
Rated PG

Directed by Phillip Noyce

Starring Everlyn Sampi, Tianna Sansbury, Laura Monaghan, Kenneth Branagh, Ningali Lawford, Myarn Lawford, David Gulpilil

THE PLOT

It's 1931 Australia and Mr. A.O. Neville (Kenneth Branagh) is the chief protector of the Aborigines. This title is ironic, since his chief task is to forcibly take half-caste Aborigine children from their mothers. This official policy is based on the government's belief that half-white children should not remain in black society. In one of his ethnic cleansing speeches, Neville claims that, "in spite of himself, the native must be helped." In the small village of Jigalong, Molly, 14 (Everlyn Sampi), Daisy, 8 (Tianna Sansbury), and Gracie, 10 (Laura Monaghan), are torn from their mother Maud (Ningali Lawford) and grandmother Frinda (Myarn Lawford). The girls are caged and shipped 1,500 miles away to Moore River Native Settlement, a "school" that would train them as domestic servants. Molly refuses to accept this enslavement: When the moment is right, she takes the younger girls and escapes. Pursued by the Aborigine tracker Moodoo (David Gulpilil) and assorted soldiers and constables, the girls walk 1,500 miles of outback in nine weeks, using the transcontinental rabbit-proof fence as their guide home. As Mr. Neville grows more and more desperate to get the girls back, the case attracts national

ISN'T HE A BIT TOO OLD FOR HER?

167

1. Ed Harris and Jennifer Connelly in *Pollock*

2. Harrison Ford and Anne Heche in *Six Days, Seven Nights*

3. Richard Gere and Winona Ryder in *Autumn in New York*

4. Dustin Hoffman and Sharon Stone in *Sphere*

5. Sam Shepard and Julia Roberts in *The Pelican Brief*

6. Bruce Willis and Amanda Peet in *The Whole Ten Yards*

7. Humphrey Bogart and Audrey Hepburn in *Sabrina*

8. Gary Cooper and Audrey Hepburn in *Love in the Afternoon*

9. Woody Allen and every leading lady since Louise Lasser

10. Michael Douglas and Gwyneth Paltrow in *A Perfect Murder*

11. Michael Douglas and Demi Moore in *Disclosure*

12. Michael Douglas and Katie Holmes in *Wonder Boys*

13. Jack Nicholson and Helen Hunt in *As Good As It Gets*

publicity. Back at Jigalong, Mother and Grandmother keep up a vigil, chanting and sending signals on the fence.

It's a road picture, a buddy flick, a thriller, and a girlhunt, packed with history and girl power. Molly even earns the respect of Moodoo, the tracker. In his only line of dialogue in the movie, he says, "This girl is clever. She wants to go home."

♥ Bonding Potential: 10

How gratifying for mothers and grandmothers to see a movie where three girls bust out of the Big House and walk 1,500 miles just to be with them. Young girls will be inspired by Molly's determina-tion—she, Gracie, and Daisy have the entire continent of Australia turned upside down (pun intended). Molly is smart, tough, and inde-pendent; she mothers the younger girls even as she longs for her own mother. At the Moore River Native Settlement, the proverbial last straw comes for Molly when she is told she has no mother. That sends her packing. When asked where she's going, Molly answers, "Home. To Mommy." Moms of 14-year-old girls: Rent this—fast.

💪 Hunk Factor: 0

As hard as it is to believe, Kenneth Branagh, who plays such a lip-less prig here, was hunky in *Henry V* and *Dead Again*.

▲ Hankie Factor: 10

Rabbit-Proof Fence is based on the book *Following the Rabbit-Proof Fence* by Doris Pilkington Garimara, Molly's daughter. Doris, like her mother and grandmother, are part of the "stolen generations" of Aus-tralia's aborigines.

BEHIND THE SCENES

Everlyn Sampi, who plays the runaway Molly, actually *did* run away during filming! She was once found hiding in a phone booth.

Also, there is a scene when Kenneth Branagh hosts a presentation to make his ridiculous case for racial purity. The slides he displays belonged to the real Mr. A. O. Neville.

AFTERMATH

This movie caused a big controversy, set off by the redoubtable Harvey Weinstein at the Cannes Film Festival. Many Australians protested its release, claiming that the children were taken from their mothers to protect them.

Tuck Everlasting (2002)
Rated PG

Directed by Jay Russell

Starring Alexis Bledel, William Hurt, Sissy Spacek, Jonathan Jackson, Scott Bairstow, Ben Kingsley, Amy Irving, Victor Garber

THE PLOT

In 1914, 16-year-old Winnie Foster (Alexis Bledel of *The Gilmore Girls*), stifled by the formality of her life, runs away into the forbidden woods. There she meets Jesse Tuck (Jonathan Jackson), and after he tells her not to drink from the spring, she is whisked away to Tuck's house by his brother Miles (Scott Bairstow). There she learns that drinking from the spring ensures immortality, keeping you forever at the same age. This explains how Jesse is 16 and 104 at the same time. Winnie stays at Jesse's house, where she connects with his mother Mae (Sissy Spacek), receives insights on the downside of immortality from his father Angus (William Hurt), and falls in love with

Jesse. She has to make a decision: Stay with Jesse forever or return home and live a normal life. In the meantime, there is the sinister Man in the Yellow Suit (Ben Kingsley), who for his own mysterious reasons is in pursuit of both the Tucks and Winnie's parents (Victor Garber and Amy Irving).

This is a young adult movie that, because of the issues raised, will appeal to everyone. Each character presents a different point of view of what it would be like to live forever. The romance between Winnie and Jesse is very sweet, and this gives their choices extra poignancy.

 Bonding Potential: 7

The themes in this movie are provocative for people of all ages. What would it mean to live forever? Would immortality be a prison sentence or a gift? Winnie's mother wants her to stay a little girl forever. In one scene we see her mother strapping her into a corset, and in another, Mae Tuck is helping her out of it. What perceptions and expectations do mothers and daughters have of one another?

 Hunk Factor: 5

Teens especially will respond to Jonathan Jackson.

Hankie Factor: 0

It's thoughtful and dramatic, but probably won't require a hankie.

 Squirming in Your Seat Watching a Sex Scene with Your Mother/Daughter Factor: 0

No squirms in the house. But there are a few sweetly romantic scenes.

BEHIND THE SCENES

Director Russell had a dream of the Man in the Yellow Suit always looking at himself in the mirror. This became his inside joke with Ben Kingsley—that when we don't see him, he's off camera looking at himself in the mirror. They picked up a shot (unscripted and unscheduled) of Ben Kingsley looking at himself in a mirror in the middle of the woods.

AFTERMATH

Ben Kingsley was knighted on New Year's Eve, 2001.

OLDER TEENS ONLY

All About My Mother (1999)
Rated R

171

Directed by Pedro Almodóvar

Starring Celia Roth, Marisa Paredes, Candela Peña, Antonia San Juan, Penelope Cruz, Rosa Maria Sardà, Eloy Azorín, Toni Cantó

THE PLOT

When her son Esteban (Eloy Azorín) dies in a car accident, Manuela (Celia Roth) heads to Madrid from Barcelona, reversing the journey she had made when she was pregnant with him. The initial trip was an effort to run away from his father (Toni Cantó), who never knew about the child. She had promised to tell Esteban all about his father, but didn't get the chance to do so before his untimely death. He wrote in his journal: "Last night Mom showed me a picture of when she was young. Half of it was missing. I didn't want to tell her, but my life is missing that same half." Now Manuela goes in search of Esteban's father to set things right and take care of her unfinished business.

In Barcelona, Manuela reconnects with her friend Agrado (Antonia San Juan), a transvestite prostitute through whom she meets Rosa (Penelope Cruz), a young pregnant nun who is headed for El Salvador. Manuela becomes the personal assistant to Huma Rojo (Marisa Paredes), an actress playing Blanche in a theater production of *A Streetcar Named Desire,* a play that has always been deeply significant in the course of Manuela's life. *All About My Mother* deals with the telling and retelling of the same story, and the redemptive, healing quality each adaptation brings.

 Bonding Potential: 3

This movie is about the many roles women play—mother, lover, friend—and how these roles define womanhood. Traditional conceptions of sexual identity are eschewed for unorthodox characters that earn our empathy and respect. There are many things for mothers and daughters to discuss, from grief to sex to transvestites.

 Hunk Factor: 2

Esteban's tall, masculine father (Toni Cantó) is oddly handsome.

 Hankie Factor: 8

Bring a jumbo-sized box of tissues.

Squirming in Your Seat Watching a Sex Scene with Your Mother/Daughter Factor: 6

There is a particularly squirmy scene at night in a field of transvestite prostitutes; all the gender-bending may make some people uncomfortable.

BEHIND THE SCENES

The movie is dedicated to the actresses of the world, and Almodóvar has said that all women are actresses. We just might agree with him.

AFTERMATH

Penelope Cruz went from playing a nun here to becoming an international star.

The Matrix (1999)
Rated R

Directed by the Wachowski brothers (Andy and Larry)

Starring Keanu Reeves, Lawrence Fishburne, Carrie-Anne Moss, Hugo Weaving, Gloria Foster, Joe Pantoliano, Marcus Chong

173

THE PLOT

Computer programmer Thomas Anderson by day, hacker Neo (Keanu Reeves) by night, is searching for an answer to the question "What is the Matrix?" The answer will help him make sense of his life. Before introducing him to Morpheus (Lawrence Fishburne), the mysterious babelicious bad-ass Trinity (Carrie-Anne Moss) tells him that the answer is out there. "It's looking for you and it will find you if you want it to." Morpheus shows him that the Matrix is a computer-generated dream world that controls the "real" real world. Everything Neo believes to be real is computerized; it is the world that has been created "to hide you from the truth." As long as the Matrix exists, the human race will never be free. The Oracle (Gloria Foster) prophesied that the return of the One would mean the destruction of the Matrix, the end of war, and freedom for real humans. Morpheus has spent his entire life looking for the One and is convinced that he found him in Neo. Morpheus and his crew (Joe Pantoliano, Marcus Chong) train Neo to fight and free his mind. "You have to let it all go, Neo—fear, doubt, disbelief. Free your mind . . . there's a difference between knowing the path and walking the path." Neo is on a journey with himself and against an enemy, led by the nefarious Agent Smith (Hugo Weaving). They fight each other with action and special effects we've never seen all in one place before. These characters are superheroes in a virtual world (or the real world . . . or whatever) who take us to the present, the future, and the post-apocalyptic worlds. They fly from wall to ceiling and from building to building as they dodge bullets and escape danger.

174

IN REAL LIFE: MATCH THE MATE (FOR NOW, ANYWAY)

1. Ryan Philippe   *a. Christine Taylor*

2. Freddie Prinze Jr.   *b. Katie Holmes*

3. Orlando Bloom   *c. Susan Levin*

4. Robert Downey Jr.   *d. Naomi Watts*

5. Josh Brolin   *e. Afton Smith*

6. Brendan Fraser   *f. Reese Witherspoon*

7. Ben Stiller   *g. Diane Lane*

8. Jake Gyllenhaal   *h. Sarah Michelle Gellar*

9. Chris Klein   *i. Kirsten Dunst*

10. Heath Ledger   *j. Kate Bosworth*

Answers: 1.(f) 2.(h) 3.(j) 4.(c) 5.(g) 6.(e) 7.(a) 8.(i) 9.(b) 10.(d)

How much are our lives limited by our own perceptions of limitation? Above the Oracle's door is a sign (in Latin, not Greek) that reads "Know Thyself." This is about the importance of knowing who and what we are, of knowing what is real and what illusion.

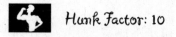 Bonding Potential: 7

For mothers out there unfamiliar with cyberspace, cyberpunk, Hong Kong action movies, and martial arts, *The Matrix* will take you into a new world. This is a new kind of movie. With elements of science fiction, action, futuristic fantasy, Buddhism, *Alice in Wonderland,* and cyberpunk parable, it is thought-provoking and visually exciting. (Warning: The plot is dense, so don't see this movie after taking medication that may cause drowsiness.) Trinity is the *true* essence of neofeminism (no pun intended). She wears shiny tight clothes, but she is smart, tough, a complete babe who doesn't cash in on her sexuality. She is a genuine role model for the cyber age.

175

Hunk Factor: 10

Keanu Reeves, Lawrence Fishburne, and Carrie-Anne Moss are the hunkiest trinity in decades.

Hankie Factor: 0

The edge of your seat will be threadbare, but you probably won't need a hankie.

 Squirming in Your Seat Watching a Sex Scene with Your Mother/Daughter Factor: 0

No sex, just loads of the other kind of action.

BEHIND THE SCENES

Wo Ping was the fight choreographer and Carrie-Anne Moss spent six months training for the opening sequence alone. According to some crew members, Keanu Reeves was really vomiting as shown in the film when his character Neo leaves the Matrix for the first time—apparently because of a chicken potpie he'd eaten.

AFTERMATH

The Wachowski brothers' contract stipulates that they would not have to do press junkets, interviews, or pose for photographs to promote *The Matrix, The Matrix Reloaded*, or *The Matrix Revolutions*. They wanted the films to speak for themselves.

On May 20, 2003, *Page Six* of the *New York Post* reported that a man named Jake Miller accused Larry Wachowski of being a cross-dresser (favoring Marilyn Monroe outfits) who stole Miller's wife, a professional dominatrix.

One True Thing (1998)
Rated R

Directed by Carl Franklin
Starring Renée Zellweger, Meryl Streep, William Hurt, Tom Everett Scott, Nicky Katt

THE PLOT

Ellen Gulden (Renée Zellweger) is a young writer living in New York; she is quite the big-city success story, working for *New York* magazine and wearing black all the time. She is hot on the trail of a major story when she returns home for a surprise party for her father, George Gulden (William Hurt), a noted professor and author. Ellen has always been under Dad's thumb, while believing her homemaker mother Kate (Meryl Streep) to be a throwback and a ditz. After the party,

Ellen and her brother Brian (Tom Everett Scott) find out that Mom has cancer. At Dad's insistence Ellen leaves New York, her job, the story, and an unfaithful boyfriend (Nicky Katt) to come home and care for Mom. Initially contemptuous of her mother's values, lifestyle, and girlfriends, Ellen gradually realizes that her mother is the strength and soul of the family.

From the beginning of time, daughters have taken their mothers for granted. It's a fact of life just like bad haircuts and cellulite. Daughters are usually more critical of their moms, too, while that enigmatic creature called Dad usually gets off with a lighter sentence. Just watch Ellen, the classic daddy's girl, relate to her mother (tone: dismissive) and then to her father (tone: obsequious). Do we expect less of our fathers? Is it Freudian? Who knows, and really, what difference does it make?

♥♥ Bonding Potential: 9

Ellen had always been somewhat condescending toward her mother. Lots of other daughters must feel the same way, because those T-shirts and birthday cards with a horrified heroine screaming, "I've turned into my mother!" have been around a long time. When Ellen begins to take care of her dying mother, to parent her, she finally sees how giving and selfless her mother has always been. "Being my mother," she admits, "is very tiring."

Dad, on the other hand, comes across as selfish, self-important, and a borderline gasbag. He has flings with coeds, too! There is a classic moment in *One True Thing*: Her father pays Ellen a great compliment—he asks her to write the introduction to his new book—and then, without missing a beat, he gives her his shirts to launder, adding "No starch."

🏋 Hunk Factor: 4

William Hurt still has that soulful look that made him so appealing in the eighties. (*One True Thing* doesn't portray Dad as a complete monster, either—we see that he really does love his wife.) Ellen's boyfriend is cute, but a bit of a womanizer, just like you know who.

 Hankie Factor: 10

You know from the beginning that Kate is going to die, but it's hard to think of a movie that depicts cancer as honestly as this one does. Don't let this scare you off—there is plenty of comedic relief in between the scenes dealing with sickness. The most poignant moment in the movie is when Kate lets Ellen know that *she* knows all about Dad: "There's nothing that you know about your father that I don't know . . . and better."

 Squirming in Your Seat Watching a Sex Scene with Your Mother/Daughter Factor: 0

BEHIND THE SCENES

Former *New York Times* columnist Anna Quindlen wrote the novel this book was based on. In real life, she, like Ellen, took a year off to care for her dying mother.

AFTERMATH

The African-American director Carl Franklin drew a perfect picture of this suburban Waspy blonde world. Meryl Streep was nominated for an Oscar, though when isn't she?

Welcome to the Dollhouse (1996)

Rated R

Directed by Todd Solondz
Starring Heather Matarazzo, Matthew Faber, Daria Kalinina, Brendan Sexton Jr., Eric
Mabius, Angela Pietropinto, Bill Buell

THE PLOT

Dawn Weiner (Heather Matarazzo) is a homely seventh grader tormented by her classmates, who call her, among other things, Lesbo and Weiner Dog. Life at home isn't any better, seeing as how her parents (Bill Buell and Angela Pietropinto) clearly prefer her obnoxious kid sister (Daria Kalinina) and smug older brother (Matthew Faber). She falls for Steve (Eric Mabius), a rock musician with a mullet that even Larry Fortensky would envy. Steve's in a rock group—using the term loosely—with Dawn's brother, and he's already posing for publicity shots. Dawn continually receives threats from the town's bad boy, Brandon (Brendan Sexton Jr.), but in time, the two realize they are soulmates.

179

It's been said the world is divided into those who loved junior high school and those who hated it. *Welcome to the Dollhouse* is definitely for those in the second camp. This movie should be depressing but it isn't, partly because it is so (darkly) funny and partly because Dawn is never defeated.

Bonding Potential: 6

It's hard to think of a movie that deals more honestly with adolescent angst and feelings of being unattractive, unpopular, and unloved. Dawn really *is* unattractive, unpopular, and unloved, and to make matters worse, she invites taunting by breathing through her mouth and wearing a Day-Glo wardrobe. At one point she asks a cheerleader, "Why do you hate me so much?" only to be flatly told, "Because you're ugly." Daughters will be moved to open up about some of the cruelty doled out by their peers.

 Hunk Factor: 0

Hankie Factor: 0

Squirming in Your Seat Watching a Sex Scene with Your Mother/Daughter Factor: 3

There may be some discomfiting moments whenever the dialogue includes the word *finger.*

BEHIND THE SCENES

The director, Todd Solondz, and the actress playing Dawn, Heather Matarazzo, look remarkably alike.

 AFTERMATH

When Solondz appeared at a panel discussion for *Welcome to the Dollhouse,* he brought along his two brothers. The contrast between the effeminate director and his macho siblings suggested that the director must have felt like Dawn growing up, an outsider in his own family.

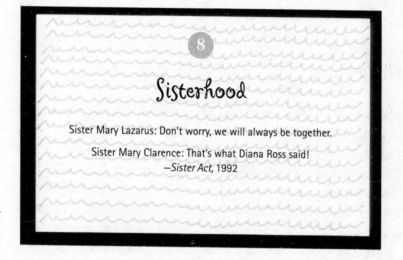

Sisterhood

Sister Mary Lazarus: Don't worry, we will always be together.

Sister Mary Clarence: That's what Diana Ross said!
—*Sister Act*, 1992

She used to pull your hair. She may have even stolen a boyfriend or two. But your sister comes with a lifetime supply of Get Out of Jail Free cards, because sisterhood is sacred and unbreakable. Even if you were born an only child or had the misfortune of being the only girl in a litter of boys, fear not, because sisters aren't always found in your family tree. Women who come to love and trust one another completely transcend friendship and become family. The following chapter celebrates the miracle of sisterhood, in its many incarnations.

Hannah and Her Sisters (1986)

Rated PG-13

Directed by Woody Allen

Starring Woody Allen, Mia Farrow, Michael Caine, Barbara Hershey, Dianne Wiest,

Maureen O'Sullivan, Lloyd Nolan

THE PLOT

The story takes place over three consecutive Thanksgivings in Manhattan. Among the three grown-up sisters, Hannah (Mia Farrow) is the stable one, Lee (Barbara Hershey) is the emotional one, and Holly (Dianne Wiest) manages to outcrazy everyone else in a cast brimming with neuroses. Try to keep up with the characters' complicated entanglements. As the film opens, Holly is recovering from cocaine abuse, and in the course of the movie, she starts and stops a couple of careers. Hannah's husband Elliot (Michael Caine) falls in love with Lee, a recovering alcoholic, and the two begin a secret affair. In the background are their sisters' bickering parents (Maureen O'Sullivan and Lloyd Nolan) and Hannah's ex-husband Mickey (Woody Allen), a TV writer who is convinced he is dying.

This is definitely one of the most screwed-up families ever to make it to the screen. At these annual homey Thanksgiving dinners, their friends find them loving and close, but beneath the surface, there's enough jealousy, betrayal, and denial to fill a Shakespearean tragedy. Or a Shakespearean comedy. Even Hannah, the "perfect" daughter, finds her life coming apart. But with all its dysfunction, the family simply can't live without each other. Despite arguments and criticism, the sisters give each other strength, love, and support, albeit each in her own way.

Bonding Potential: 5

Okay, you daughters out there, you might as well learn, sooner rather than later, that the day will come when you will be the parent to your mother. In one scene, Hannah rushes to care for her mother (Maureen O'Sullivan), who is coming off a drunken bender. Hannah has to listen to the old boozehound mourn her lost career and berate her husband (Lloyd Nolan) for his fancy haircuts. Hannah looks at pictures of her parents when they were young and beautiful, and in an interior monologue, she tries to understand when and why they got so lost.

 Hunk Factor: 1

Younger viewers should be informed that, in his younger, skinnier *Alfie* days, Michael Caine was quite a hunk.

 Hankie Factor: 0

183

 Squirming in Your Seat Watching a Sex Scene with Your Mother/Daughter Factor: 0

BEHIND THE SCENES

In her autobiography, Mia Farrow claimed that Woody in real life lusted after her sister Tisa. In another art-imitating-life scenario, Mia's real mother, Maureen O'Sullivan, played her mother, and several of Mia's children appeared in the movie, including her daughters Dylan and Soon-Yi.

AFTERMATH

There is a scene in the movie when a censor wants to edit Mickey's writing, telling him, "Child molestation is a tricky subject." Mickey, played by Woody Allen, responds, "What do you mean—half the country is do-ing it!" Seven years later, there was a major scandal when Woody left Mia for her adopted daughter Soon-Yi. It got even messier when Mia ac-cused Woody of molesting their young daughter Dylan. Mia alleged that Woody's values were the opposite of those he put forth in *Hannah and Her Sisters:* "What rage did he feel against me, against women, against mothers, against sisters, against daughters, against an entire family?"

Little Women (1994)
Rated PG

Directed by Gillian Armstrong

Starring Winona Ryder, Susan Sarandon, Gabriel Byrne, Kirsten Dunst, Eric Stoltz, Claire Danes, Samantha Mathis, Trini Alvarado, Christian Bale

THE PLOT

The benevolent Marmee March (Susan Sarandon) raises her four daughters alone while her husband is serving in the Civil War. The sisters, though wildly different in nature, are as close as siblings can be. Meg (Trini Alvarado), the eldest, is sweet and proper; Jo (Winona Ryder) is independent and outspoken; Beth (Claire Danes), after sur-viving scarlet fever, is sickly; and Amy (Kirsten Dunst/Samantha Mathis) is artistic and energetic. Neighbor Laurie (Christian Bale) is quite taken with the girls, particularly Jo, and becomes a fixture in the March household. *Little Women* traces the lives of these girls as they grow into women, and we see the four sisters stand by one an-other through war, heartbreak, and death. It is a celebration of the force of nature that is sisterhood.

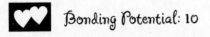 *Bonding Potential:* 10

There is plenty of bonding material here, as the March sisters will allow nothing to come between them. Their code of sisterhood is

something we women can all aspire to whether we have blood sisters or not. Such strong familial values were surely instilled in the siblings by their beloved Marmee, she of the quiet strength and aproned frock. She never seems to make a false step, even during exceedingly difficult times. One would think that this might get annoying, but thankfully she remains just shy of in-your-face flawlessness. Without preaching, she teaches her "little women" to discover their own true north. She is certainly a hard act for real mothers to follow.

 Hunk Factor: 8

What's not to love about Christian Bale? That couldn't have been him in *American Psycho,* could it? We love Gabriel Byrne, too, though he does seem a tad too old for Winona.

 Hankie Factor: 9

Get 'em out, girls. Better yet, just buy a family-sized box of Kleenex.

 Squirming in Your Seat Watching a Sex Scene with Your Mother/Daughter Factor: 0

BEHIND THE SCENES

During filming, Claire Danes's hair caught on fire while she was carrying a candle up the stairs.

AFTERMATH

This is the eighth and best cinematic adaptation of Louisa May Alcott's novel *Little Women,* following four movie and three TV versions. It should be pointed out that this is the only one directed by a woman.

Pride and Prejudice (1996)

Not rated

Directed by Simon Langton

Starring Jennifer Ehle, Colin Firth, Susannah Harker, Crispin Bonham Carter, Alison Steadman, Benjamin Whitrow, Adrian Lukis, Julia Sawalha, David Bamber

THE PLOT

This is the latest adaptation of Jane Austen's classic, and our favorite. Mr. and Mrs. Bennet (Alison Steadman and Benjamin Whitrow) have five daughters but very little money for their daughters' dowries. Their eldest, Jane (Susannah Harker), and the wealthy Mr. Bingley (Crispin Bonham Carter) fall in love, but the proud, haughty Mr. Darcy (Colin Firth) convinces Bingley that Jane is unworthy of him. When her sister Elizabeth (Jennifer Ehle) learns about this, she blames Mr. Darcy for breaking her sister's heart. Despite her open prejudice toward him, Mr. Darcy finds himself being drawn to the strong-willed, outspoken Elizabeth.

Don't get us wrong: We love the 1940 film with Laurence Olivier and Greer Garson, but this BBC/A&E production is three hours longer, making it a fully realized version of the novel. Also, it's filmed in the stately homes of England instead of on a Hollywood back lot. The final argument against the 1940 version is that the 36-year-old Greer Garson played 20-year-old Elizabeth Bennet as opposed to the more age appropriate Jennifer Ehle. Laurence Olivier, however, was equally divine as Colin Firth in the role of Mr. Darcy.

186

Bonding Potential: 10

Attention, moms and daughters: Put the kettle on, grab that afghan, bake some chewy cookies, and cuddle together for 270 minutes of pure bliss. One of the silliest mothers ever to show up in a book or movie, Mrs. Bennet spends most of her time blabbering, blubbering blithering, and swooning. Elizabeth Bennet, her daughter, is the opposite: Strong and independent, she resists Mom's attempt to marry her off, declaring, "I am determined that nothing but the deepest love could ever induce me into matrimony."

 Hunk Factor: 9

Colin Firth, particularly in the scene when he gets off his horse and cools off with a swim!

 Hankie Factor: 0

 Squirming in Your Seat Watching a Sex Scene with Your Mother/Daughter Factor: 0

BEHIND THE SCENES

Jane Austen, the most adapted author at the end of the twentieth century, never married and stayed home all the time. So it's fitting that *Pride and Prejudice* induced millions to stay home, too . . . it made ratings history for both BBC and A&E.

AFTERMATH

Helen Fielding had both Mr. Darcy and Colin Firth in mind when she created the character of Mark Darcy in *Bridget Jones's Diary*. When the *Bridget Jones* movie was made, Colin Firth played this adapted Mr. Darcy.

Sense and Sensibility (1995)

Rated PG

Directed by Ang Lee

Starring Emma Thompson, Kate Winslet, Alan Rickman, Hugh Grant, Greg Wise, James Fleet

THE PLOT

Mr. Dashwood dies and his estate passes to his male heir, a son by his first marriage. This leaves his widow and three daughters penniless and forced to move from their home. Elinor (Emma Thompson), the eldest, takes charge of her family, and though she is all sense, she nevertheless falls in love with the shy Mr. Ferrars (Hugh Grant). Her sister and emotional opposite, Marianne (Kate Winslet), is all sensibility, and she has a fling with Willoughby (Greg Wise). In the meantime, Marianne's new neighbor, Brandon (Alan Rickman), suffers from unrequited love for her.

The late 1990s were marked by a fascination with the early nineteenth-century world of Jane Austen. Besides this movie, there was *Clueless, Emma, Pride and Prejudice, Persuasion,* and *Mansfield Park.* Austen's world of manners and silent suffering strangely resonates in our age of psychobabble and self-expression. She recalls a world where everybody obsesses over money, particularly when they don't seem to have a lot of it. It's good to know that some things never change. Back then, the only way women who weren't born rich could get their mitts on money was to marry it. But marrying money was particularly difficult for Austen's heroines because then, like nowadays, rich people tended to stick together.

♥♥ Bonding Potential: 8

Maybe mothers and daughters would behave better toward each other if they called each other "dearest" all the time, like the women

BAD GIRLS

1. Elizabeth Shue,* *Leaving Las Vegas*

2. Susan Sarandon, *Pretty Baby*

3. Brooke Shields,* *Pretty Baby*

4. Gwyneth Paltrow, *Hard Eight*

5. Jane Fonda,* *Klute*

6. Melanie Griffith, *Milk Money*

7. Elizabeth Taylor, *Butterfield 8*

8. Jodie Foster,* *Taxi Driver*

9. Jean Harlow, *Red Dust*

10. Rita Hayworth, *Miss Sadie Thompson*

11. Julia Roberts, *Pretty Woman*

12. Julie Christie, *McCabe and Mrs. Miller*

13. Barbra Streisand, *Nuts*

14. Mira Sorvino,* *Mighty Aphrodite*

15. Patricia Arquette, *True Romance*

*Indicates Ivy League Education

in *Sense and Sensibility.* We like to think so, at least. Moms could learn a thing or two from Mrs. Dashwood, since her daughters spend most of the film trying to protect *her.* The Dashwood women really are a family and they survive because they have one another.

Outwardly, the collected females seem to do nothing more than drink tea while the men head off to London, always, it seems, on some important mission. But by the conclusion of *Sense and Sensibility,* it becomes evident which is the stronger sex. The men are weak and mopey, and one—the cutest, naturally—is a downright rat. The women, seemingly so powerless, are really in control. In fact, it's the stingy Fanny, the Dashwoods' sister-in-law, who sets the plot in motion.

(NB: In the course of this movie, Elinor is called a spinster. Young girls should give thanks that this word with all its pinched, dried-up connotations has mercifully fallen out of fashion.)

  Hunk Factor: 4

Alan Rickman, Marianne's rich-but-long-in-the-tooth suitor, really does have long teeth! Hugh Grant, the man with the famous stammer, is charming as always, as he tugs at his trademark floppy hair. The film's official hunk award goes to Greg Wise as the dashing Willoughby; we know what Marianne is talking about when she says, "What care I for colds when there is such a man."

Hankie Factor: 2

Particularly during a mortal crisis when, fittingly, Elinor calls for her mother.

Ah, the beauty of watching Jane Austen with your mother or daughter.

BEHIND THE SCENES

Oddly, this film about romantic heartbreak coincided with Emma Thompson's divorce from actor Kenneth Branagh. He went on to canoodle with Helena Bonham Carter.

AFTERMATH

Emma Thompson's excellent screenplay was nominated for an Oscar.

OLDER TEENS ONLY

Manny and Lo (1996)
Rated R

Directed by Lisa Krueger
Starring Scarlett Johansson, Aleksa Palladino, Mary Kay Place, Paul Guilfoyle

THE PLOT

After their mother dies, 11-year-old Manny (Scarlett Johansson) and 16-year-old Lo (Aleksa Palladino) leave their foster families and hit the road in a stolen car. The sisters squat in unoccupied model homes, shoplift food, and check for their pictures on milk cartons. When Lo finally confronts the fact that she is pregnant, she is denied an abortion from a local clinic because she's too far along in her pregnancy. Lo storms out of the clinic, still in the paper gown, and the girls realize they need help. This prompts them to wonder what advice Mom would give if she were around:

> *Manny:* What would Mom tell us?
> *Lo:* Depends. Is she drunk or stoned?

They see Elaine (Mary Kay Place), a clerk in a baby store who for no apparent reason wears a nurse's uniform on the job. Manny and Lo, convinced Elaine is a baby expert, kidnap her and bring her to a vacant cottage in the country. They tie a bike chain around her ankles and keep her in captivity. Despite such an unorthodox introduction to the sisters, Elaine gradually takes charge of their lives. Manny asks, "Did you ever dream about someone before you saw them in life?" Unbeknownst to all involved, the girls have been waiting for Elaine and Elaine has been waiting for them.

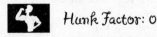 Bonding Potential: 8

We all need a mother. Manny and Lo's mother was an addict and a drunk who kept dumping them in foster homes. Still, the sisters spray their sheets with Arrid Extra Dry because it reminds them of her. When they find Elaine, she's an odd mother figure to be sure, but a mother figure nonetheless. It's hard not to laugh watching her shuffle around the house (her ankles *are* chained), preparing home-cooked meals and spouting homey platitudes.

We all need a family, too. Elaine has been kidnapped, and it turns out, nobody cares. Nobody looks for her, not even her church group! She needs the girls just as much as they need her. By the end of the film mothers and daughters will find themselves marveling at the splendid symbiosis that is family.

Hunk Factor: 0

The only men are Lo's pubescent boyfriend, the driver of a monster truck, and the frumpy owner of the house.

Hankie Factor: 2

A baby is born, which is always good for a hankie or two.

 Squirming in Your Seat Watching a Sex Scene with Your Mother/Daughter Factor: 2

Some grunting, some gurgling, and lots of profanity.

BEHIND THE SCENES

Director Lisa Krueger developed *Manny and Lo* at the Sundance Film Institute.

AFTERMATH

Scarlett Johanssen went on to be a star, but why isn't Mary Kay Place in more movies?

193

The Virgin Suicides (2000)
Rated PG-13

Directed by Sofia Coppola
Starring Kirsten Dunst, James Woods, Kathleen Turner, Josh Hartnett, Michael Paré, Danny DeVito, Hanna Hall

THE PLOT

It's the mid-seventies and the five Lisbon sisters live in a Detroit suburb under the strict supervision of their repressed parents, Mr. and Mrs. Lisbon (James Woods and Kathleen Turner). The neighborhood boys are in love with these sheltered, enigmatic beauties, and to the best of their abilities, they keep detailed track of their lives. They are most captivated by Lux (Kirsten Dunst), the most haunting and luminous of the flawless, blonde sisters.

At 13, Cecilia (Hanna Hall) is the youngest, and as one of the boys puts it "was the first to go." Some time after Cecilia's suicide, the high school stud Tripp Fontaine (Josh Hartnett) and Lux fall for each other. Tripp convinces her parents to let him take Lux to the prom by offering to find dates for the other sisters. You'd better believe Mrs. Lisbon designed the most conservative dresses for this occasion, and Mr. Lisbon himself was a chaperon to the event. Despite their cautious measures, Lux stays out all night, prompting her parents to abruptly pull all four remaining sisters from school.

You can figure out from the title that there is no life after high school for the Lisbon girls, but still, the movie is not all that depressing. Since it's narrated by the neighborhood boys, it begins to feel like a dream, and you sometimes wonder if the girls are real or products of their fevered imagination. *The Virgin Suicides* also manages to be quite funny, particularly when the parents (who become increasingly psychotic) are onscreen. In one scene, Mr. Lisbon talks to his plants: "Have we photosynthesized our breakfast today?"

 Bonding Potential: 8

After the youngest Lisbon girl has her first, failed suicide attempt, her parents take her to a psychiatrist (Danny DeVito), the only enlightened thing they do in the whole movie. The shrink dismissively tells her, "You're not even old enough to know how hard life gets." Cecilia answers for all of us who suffered through early adolescence: "Obviously, Doctor, you've never been a 13-year-old girl." Though the Lisbon girls are paragons of blonde perfection, at 13, we're all Dawn Weiner (*Welcome to the Dollhouse*) in one way or another.

We know you moms out there want to keep your daughters as young as you can for as long as you can. But accept the fact that in the fight against hormones, the hormones usually win. Don't turn into Mrs. Lisbon: To deny her daughters' sexual awakening, she keeps them from boys and movies and imposes religion, nature programs on TV, and frumpy prom dresses on them. Just look how that ended up.

 ### Hunk Factor: 8

We spotted potential hunkitude in Josh Hartnett and predicted that he would go on to be a big star. He is especially endearing when lovesick; at one point he tells Lux, "You are a stone fox," and we believed him! Whatever-Happened-to-Hunk Michael Paré plays Tripp Fontaine as an adult.

 ### Hankie Factor: 1

The opening line gives the ending away: "Everybody dates the decline of our neighborhood to the deaths of the Lisbon girls." Maybe it's knowing that the girls are doomed that prevents *The Virgin Suicides* from being distressing or depressing. It is, however, quite moving.

Squirming in Your Seat Watching a Sex Scene with Your Mother/Daughter Factor: 2

BEHIND THE SCENES

Sofia Coppola was concerned about the effect a movie about teen suicide might have on young audiences. She checked with the National Association of Suicide Prevention, who assured her that you couldn't put this idea into someone's head and it would be good to open up conversation on the topic, which most parents avoid talking or thinking about.

AFTERMATH

We saw *Godfather III,* Sofia Coppola's acting debut (and finale), in the movie theater. Every time Sofia opened her mouth, the audience dissolved in laughter, poor girl. But with the critical and commercial success of *The Virgin Suicides* and 2003's *Lost in Translation,* she got the proverbial last laugh.

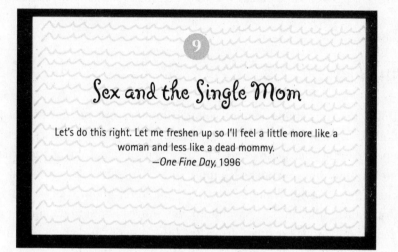

9

Sex and the Single Mom

Let's do this right. Let me freshen up so I'll feel a little more like a
woman and less like a dead mommy.
—*One Fine Day*, 1996

Single moms don't have it easy. It's hard enough to juggle
parenting and working, not to mention finding the time and energy for a love life. And then there's the ever-elusive luxury
called privacy. Still, girls—even single moms—just wanna have
fun. See how some of the following movie moms managed to live
the dream: part soccer mom, part sex goddess, these women
will bring hope to the most frazzled of mothers.

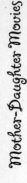

Anywhere but Here (1999)

Rated PG-13

Directed by Wayne Wang

Starring Susan Sarandon, Natalie Portman, Hart Bochner, Shawn Hatosy, Bonnie Bedelia, Corbin Allred

THE PLOT

Hollywood has made a mini–cottage industry out of movies about flighty, dramatic mothers with serious, put-upon daughters. Once upon a time this genre had the dignified designation of maternal melodrama, but nowadays it's more often demeaned as some kind of chick flick. Wayne Wang's *Anywhere but Here,* about, yes, a flighty, dramatic mother (Susan Sarandon) who moves her serious, put-upon daughter (Natalie Portman) from Bay City, Wisconsin, to Beverly Hills, transcends its chick flick clichés thanks to the presence of two uncommonly good actresses. As Adele August, Susan Sarandon dresses as if she's painted on the side of a B-52 bomber and in her nutty, pathetic histrionics channels the spirit of Mama Rose. But Sarandon also imbues the character with a ferocious and passionate (if somewhat misguided) optimism, not to mention a mother lion's love for her child. Natalie Portman plays daughter Ann, and of the two, Portman does work that is more inward and more remarkable by far. She conveys a quiet strength and deserves a special Oscar for best performance that should have been sappy but wasn't.

Based on Mona Simpson's acclaimed novel, *Anywhere but Here* is a funny, heartfelt portrait of a very complex relationship between mother and daughter. As to the plot, they mostly fight, then go get ice cream. In the meantime, however, boyfriends are found and lost, Christmases ruined, lessons learned, and many miles driven in Adele's beat-up gold Mercedes.

Bonding Potential: 7

Anywhere but Here seems tailor-made for mothers to watch with their teenage daughters. Though Adele and Ann are at the crazy end of the relationship spectrum, when things get tough for them, they love and support each other. Throughout the course of the film, Adele's selfishness gives way to self-sacrifice, and Ann's melancholy gives way to maturity. "Doesn't she know I would do anything for her? I love her. She is the reason I was born," says Adele in the film's climactic moment. By the end, Adele has become the mother Ann always needed and wanted.

 ### Hunk Factor: 7

Shawn Hatosy plays Ann's sweet but slightly dim cousin and best friend, and frankly we find their relationship a tad suspect. And Corbin Allred plays her trumpet-playing T. S. Eliot–quoting *90210* boyfriend. They're both kind and cute enough to compensate for Adele's beau hunk Josh, who "is more than just a dentist . . . He's writing a screenplay."

 ### Hankie Factor: 7

Between the film's many tragic scenes and the evocative Lillith Fair soundtrack, not to mention the heartwarming ending, it should be pretty difficult to maintain one's composure.

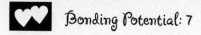 ### Squirming in Your Seat Watching a Sex Scene with Your Mother/Daughter Factor: 3

BEHIND THE SCENES

Susan Sarandon agreed to be in this film only if Natalie Portman would play her daughter.

AFTERMATH

Susan Sarandon is often denounced for her leftist politics. Natalie Portman will be once more dabbling in intergalactic politics in 2005 in the third *Star Wars* prequel.

Chocolat (2000)
Rated PG-13

Directed by Lasse Hallström
Starring Juliette Binoche, Johnny Depp, Lena Olin, Alfred Molina, Judi Dench, Leslie
Caron, Carrie-Anne Moss, Peter Stormare, Victoire Thivisol

THE PLOT

Vianne (Juliette Binoche) and her 6-year-old daughter Anouk (Victoire Thivisol) blow into town, literally, and make their home in a 1950s French village. In this fable, mother and daughter open a *chocolaterie,* shocking the townspeople, most particularly the puritanical mayor (Alfred Molina), because they've set up shop at the beginning of Lent. Vianne peddles her chocolate to a collection of locals and soon the repressed village is awash in sensuousness and romance. She takes in an abused wife (Lena Olin) and a landlady (Judi Dench) who doesn't get along with her prissy daughter (Carrie-Anne Moss). If Vianne weren't enough for the village prudes, along comes Roux (Johnny Depp) and his band of Irish river gypsies.

We know Vianne is a freethinker right away—check out those red high heels! Vianne and her daughter are descended from a hot-blooded Mayan who handed down the secret to unleashing the sensual power of chocolate. No wonder they are instantly pitted against the forces of prudery, repression, and religious hypocrisy.

 ## Bonding Potential: 8

Anouk, closely bound to her mother, still goes through that phase that every daughter experiences: She wants her mom to be just like the other moms. Anouk thinks Vianne should go to church and wear sensible shoes. Vianne handles her daughter's rebellion with some inspired wisdom—not easy for a woman who's an unrepentant unwed mom, who may in fact be a pagan priestess. We know that Vianne's independence and courage has won out when Anouk sits and gambles with a bunch of curmudgeonly old men, who represent the paternalistic and sexist attitude of the village. She wins.

 ## Hunk Factor: 10

Johnny Depp is smoldering as the funky-coiffed Irishman.

Hankie Factor: 4

The weepy parts work, thanks to Dame Judi.

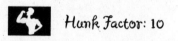 ## Squirming in Your Seat Watching a Sex Scene with Your Mother/Daughter Factor: 0

BEHIND THE SCENES

When chocolate was introduced to France in the 1600s, it was considered a dangerous drug. Personally, we think they were right. So you better stock up on a giant box of SnoCaps (is there any other kind?) when you settle in to watch this movie.

Also, Lena Olin, who plays the abused wife, is the real-life wife of the director, Lasse Hallström.

AFTERMATH

The movie was nominated for five Academy Awards, including best picture.

Indochine (1992)
Rated PG-13

Directed by Régis Wargnier
Starring Catherine Deneuve, Vincent Perez, Linh Dan Pham, Jean Yanne, Dominique
Blanc, Henri Marteau, Carlo Brandt

THE PLOT

In Colonial Vietnam, wealthy French landowner Eliane (Catherine Deneuve) is raising Indo-Chinese Camille (Linh Dan Pham), the daughter of her late friends. Eliane has a brief, secret affair with a young French navy officer, Jean-Baptiste (Vincent Perez). As fate would have it, Camille, ignorant of her mother's history with him, falls in love with Jean-Baptiste and is sure that in time he will love her, too. To keep her former flame from her adopted daughter, the protective Eliane has him transferred to a beautiful yet isolated outpost in Northern Vietnam. Strong-willed Camille sets out to find him, and when she does, the two fall deeply in love. After a series of wrong place/wrong time moments, the couple is separated, and Camille is sent to prison, which is where her burgeoning Marxist beliefs take root.

The story is told from Eliane's perspective, making it more a story of European imperialism than of cultural revolution. Both women are symbols of the geopolitical changes: The controlling, wealthy, land-owning mother is France and the daughter, desperate for her independence, represents Vietnam. Just like Eliane and Camille, the French and Vietnamese worlds are mixed together, but also like the two women, these cultures never become a cohesive whole.

 Bonding Potential: 6

Even though the mother-daughter relationship is not completely explored, a lot is going on between and around them, not the least of which is loving the same man. The film is a romantic commentary on

WARNING: DO *NOT* SEE WITH YOUR MOTHER OR YOUR DAUGHTER

1. *Basic Instinct*

2. *Swept Away* (1974)

3. *Snoop Dogg's Huslaz: Diary of a Pimp*

4. *Body Heat*

5. *Y Tu Mamá También*

6. *Last Tango in Paris*

7. *Eat Drink Man Woman*

8. *Secretary*

9. *Henry and June*

10. *Unfaithful*

imperialism, wealth, poverty, mothers, and daughters. Finally, and at the risk of sounding shallow, we think moms and daughters will love *Indochine*'s gorgeous wardrobe.

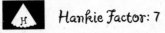 Hunk Factor: 10

Vincent Perez as Jean-Baptiste is the hunk most worthy ever of being fought over by a mother and daughter.

![Hankie Factor icon] Hankie Factor: 7

There is a reunion moment toward the end of the movie that is trés tragique.

![Squirming icon] Squirming in Your Seat Watching a Sex Scene with Your Mother/Daughter Factor: 7

While there is not an abundance of skin, the love scenes we see are romantic and sexually charged.

BEHIND THE SCENES

Indochine was shot in France, Malaysia, and Vietnam. Vincent Perez, who romanced the older woman Catherine Deneuve onscreen, was seriously involved in real life with another older woman, Jacqueline Bisset.

AFTERMATH

Catherine Deneuve won her first and only Academy Award nomination for best actress. She didn't win the Oscar but did win the French equivalent, a César.

Mermaids (1990)
Rated PG-13

Directed by Richard Benjamin
Starring Cher, Winona Ryder, Christina Ricci, Bob Hoskins, Michael Schoeffling

THE PLOT

It's 1962. A free-spirited single mom with two daughters, Mrs. Flax (Cher) moves around a lot, skipping town before her sexy reputation catches up with her. The narrator of the story is 15-year-old Charlotte (Winona Ryder), who's in love with saints and all things Catholic, even though the family is Jewish. Kate (Christina Ricci), 9, is a swimming champ; she is eccentric too, preferring to keep her swim cap on most of the time. They settle in a small town in Massachusetts, in a house close to a convent, a fact that delights Charlotte. Charlotte's ardor gets redirected, however, when she falls for the convent's caretaker, Joe (Michael Schoeffling). Mom gets a new boyfriend, Lou (Bob Hoskins), who wants to make them all into a "normal" family, but as usual, Mrs. Flax is afraid of commitment.

All moms embarrass their daughters some of the time. Mrs. Flax embarrasses Charlotte *all* of the time. She is the only mother in town who wears tight dresses, heavy makeup, and backless high heels, and serves nothing but "fun finger foods" for dinner. This is particularly hard for Charlotte, who aspires to be a saint, or at the very least, a nun: "I try to be charitable, taking care of Kate and not killing my mother."

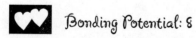 Bonding Potential: 8

Even though this is a pretty zany family, Charlotte and Mrs. Flax are like most mothers and teenage daughters—at odds with each other a lot of the time. There's a particularly funny scene when Charlotte criticizes her mother and Mrs. Flax responds with "We're going to play our favorite game, 'Who's the Worst Mother in the Whole Wide World?' Oh, no, no, don't tell me. Let me guess—who could it be? Could it be meeeee?" Charlotte laughs. Moms, try to remember that one.

You can say a lot of things about Mrs. Flax, but her honesty makes her sympathetic. What parent wouldn't identify with her line "Sometimes being the mother really stinks. You and your sister didn't come with a book of instructions."

 Hunk Factor: 5

Michael Schoeffling is hunky, inspiring this prayer of Charlotte's: "Please, God, don't let me fall in love and want to do disgusting things!" Anyone know what ever happened to him?

Hankie Factor: 0

 Squirming in Your Seat Watching a Sex Scene with Your Mother/Daughter Factor: 0

BEHIND THE SCENES

Cher based her portrayal of Mrs. Flax on her own mother, Georgia Holt, an astrologist who was married six times. Pardon our skepticism, but Mrs. Holt claims to have given birth to Cher when she was 13.

AFTERMATH

This was the first movie for Christina Ricci, who quickly went on to make dozens more. Right after Cher finished *Mermaids,* she made her biggest professional blunder: She starred in an infomercial for a line of hair-care products, a move she delicately summarized by saying, "There's nothing like an infomercial to slam-dunk your ass."

Mostly Martha (2002)

Rated PG

Directed by Sandra Nettelbeck

Starring Martina Gedeck, Maxime Foerste, Sergio Castellitto, August Zirner, Sibylle Canonica, Katja Studt

THE PLOT

Before there was *The Restaurant,* there was Martha. No, not *that* Martha. We're talking about Martha (Martina Gedeck) of *Mostly Martha,* a workaholic celebrity chef in a Hamburg restaurant. She is

TRANSFORMATIONS

	Before	After
Demi Moore	*Ghost*	*GI Jane*
Melanie Griffith	*Working Girl*	*Crazy in Alabama*
Paul Newman	*The Verdict*	*Road to Perdition*
Barbara Hershey	*The Right Stuff*	*Beaches*
Nicolas Cage	*Rumble Fish*	*Adaptation*
Cher	*Silkwood*	*Tea with Mussolini*
Madelyn Stowe	*Short Cuts*	*We Were Soldiers*
Montgomery Clift	*Raintree County*	*Raintree County*

single with a serious attitude problem: She seldom speaks except to talk about food, and retreats from her coworkers by hiding in the freezer. Such behavior has prompted her boss Frida (Sibylle Canonica) to insist Martha see a shrink. After her sister is killed in a car accident, Martha takes in her 8-year-old niece, Lina (Maxime Foerste), until she can locate the girl's father. Lina is depressed and sullen, and worse, she doesn't like Martha's cooking. Into this mix comes Mario (Sergio Castellitto), an Italian sous-chef newly hired at the restaurant. Martha is threatened by Mario's Italian brio, his earthy approach to food, music, and life, but her sullen niece embraces him.

A case could be made for calling *Mostly Martha* a foodie and female version of *About a Boy*. In both films, headstrong solitary adults have their lives upended by headstrong solitary children. The grown-ups only *appear* to be in charge; it's the kids who take over and finally help them to engage in life.

 Bonding Potential: 9

Martha's life is ordered, precise—okay, Teutonic—until Lina moves in, making a mess of everything. Moms in the audience might be tempted to yell at the screen, "Martha! When you have kids, life is messy!" We see her discover that perfectionism and parenthood is a bad—nay, impossible mix.

Daughters watching Martha's makeshift babysitting arrangements can see how working moms juggle childcare arrangements. It's not easy.

Hunk Factor: 1

There is Mario, and Martha's downstairs neighbor, Sam. Both seem to have great personalities (if you know what we mean).

Hankie Factor: 0

BEHIND THE SCENES

None of the actors playing chefs knew how to cook. Famed chef Rocco Dressel was hired to give a series of culinary lessons to the cast.

AFTERMATH

Director Nettelbeck won the Grand Prix at the International Women's Film Festival.

Mr. Skeffington (1944)
Not rated

Directed by Vincent Sherman
Starring Bette Davis, Claude Rains, Walter Abel, Richard Waring, Marjorie Riordan

THE PLOT

Fanny Trellis (Bette Davis) is the most beautiful woman in New York. She has lots of admirers, but her heart belongs to her shiftless brother, Trippy (Richard Waring). Her brother's employer, Job Skeffington (Claude Rains), as besotted by Fanny as every other man, tells her that Trippy has stolen money from him. Fanny can't pay the money back, so she marries Mr. Skeffington to prevent her brother from going to prison. Trippy, disgusted by her marriage, goes off to World War I in a huff; he is soon killed. The Skeffingtons have a daughter, Young Fanny, and when they divorce, Fanny cheerfully gives her husband custody. Years pass. Fanny contracts diphtheria and loses her fabled looks. When trouble starts brewing in Europe, Young Fanny (Marjorie Riordan) must return to her mother in the United States.

This is one of the great woman's pictures of the 1940s. The unconventional-looking (at best) Miss Bette Davis convinces us that she really is the greatest beauty of her day. Our favorite scene is when a gentleman caller meets mother and daughter for the first time. He says to the daughter, "I think I'll call you 'Young Fanny,'" then turns to Mom, saying, "And I'll call you 'Ol—'" Oops—it's sure hard getting old! Or, as Bette Davis put it, "Old age is not for sissies."

 Bonding Potential: 5

Poor Young Fanny: It isn't until her mother loses her looks that she is able to relate to her daughter. Moms, please! Don't wait until you catch diphtheria, start balding, and are forced to wear three inches of face powder before you bond with your daughter. We know from *Mildred Pierce* that old movies can hit at sexual tension between mothers and daughters. Young Fanny runs off with Mom's boyfriend—the only one that was cute, too!

 Hunk Factor: 0

By the way, if she's so beautiful, why couldn't she get better-looking boyfriends?

Hankie Factor: 8

Job comes back, devastated by World War II. He's blind—good thing because he doesn't get to see his ex-wife looking like the character she played in *What Ever Happened to Baby Jane?* When he tells Fanny, "A woman is beautiful only when she is loved," we almost believe him. Get ready to grab that hankie.

 **Squirming in Your Seat Watching a Sex Scene with Your Mother/Daughter Factor: 0**

BEHIND THE SCENES

There was still a war on, and Bette stayed busy organizing the Hollywood Canteen, entertaining GIs even while she was making this movie.

AFTERMATH

She was also busy fighting with her studio over her contract and refused to start *Mr. Skeffington* until her demands were met. Maybe this prompted her observation: "Until you're known in my profession as a monster, you're not a star."

Tumbleweeds (1999)

Rated PG-13

Directed by Gavin O'Connor
Starring Janet McTeer, Jay O. Sanders, Kimberly J. Brown, Gavin O'Connor, Laurel Holloman, Lois Smith, Michael J. Pollard

THE PLOT

The movie opens with Mary Jo (Janet McTeer) and Ava (Kimberly J. Brown) escaping an abusive husband/father. They are a great pair. Mary Jo is smarter and spunkier than the traditional blue-collar men she takes up with, but her sexuality is her currency and her means of survival. That is, until she meets Dan (Jay O. Sanders), a kind widower who is more interested in getting to know Mary Jo personally than biblically.

According to the director, there is absolutely no plot. Instead, it's a peek into the lives of a mother and daughter who are perpetually on the road, bouncing from one man's world to the next. It is the semi-autobiographical story of writer Angela Shelton and her mother, who traversed the country eleven times, their departures and arrivals always motivated by men. In reality, mother and daughter are said to love and adore each other; this also comes through in the story.

Bonding Potential: 10

This mother-daughter road movie is a bonding fest. It is far from traditional, with their relationship shifting from being like mother and daughter to being like sisters. This is clearly illustrated when Mary Jo helps Ava prepare for her first date. Like a sister, she helps Ava look fetching, but when Ava leaves, Mary Jo breaks down in tears at the thought of her baby growing up.

Hunk Factor: 0

Only tumbleweeds on the horizon, no hotties in sight.

Hankie Factor: 0

 Squirming in Your Seat Watching a Sex Scene with Your Mother/Daughter Factor: 5

There is one very squirmy scene when 12-year-old Ava walks in on Mary Jo and Dan, but then again, the whole concept of a mother migrating from one way station of a man to another is squirmy in itself.

BEHIND THE SCENES

The tall (six-one) Janet McTeer was nominated for an Oscar and won the Golden Globe for best actress in 2000. Her wardrobe for the whole movie cost around $200.

AFTERMATH

Director O'Connor says of *Tumbleweeds*, "Ultimately it is a love story between a mother and a daughter." He dedicated the movie to Angela and her mother.

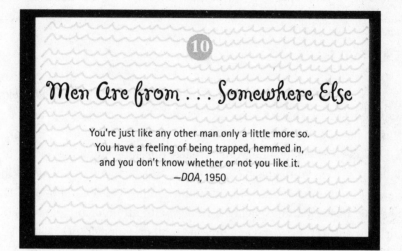

10

Men Are from . . . Somewhere Else

You're just like any other man only a little more so.
You have a feeling of being trapped, hemmed in,
and you don't know whether or not you like it.
—*DOA*, 1950

They say we women are mysterious beings. Well, we think men are harder to solve than the (London) *Sunday Times* crossword puzzle. Whether it's Dad, the grouchy next-door neighbor, or the boy who sat next to you in geometry, the opposite sex sure can be hard to decipher. Males behave erratically: sometimes badly, sometimes nobly. They can be insensitive, but easy to offend. They can burp at will (okay, so can we, but we're not as proud of it). It's hard to get them to talk about what they're really thinking, unless it's about sports. And, by the way, what's so hard about remembering to put the toilet seat down? Here are some movies that might shed some light on the curious figures known as men.

About a Boy (2002)
Rated PG-13

Directed by Chris Weitz and Paul Weitz

Starring Hugh Grant, Toni Collette, Nicholas Hoult, Rachel Weisz, Sharon Small

THE PLOT

The appropriately named Will Freeman (Hugh Grant) is 38, a bachelor so self-absorbed that he insists to his disbelieving friends, "I really *am* this shallow." He's never had a serious relationship or, for that matter, a job; he derives his income from a treacly Christmas tune penned by his late father. Will fabricates a child to join SPAT (Single Parents Alone Together) in the hope of meeting available women. Instead he meets 12-year-old misfit Marcus (Nicholas Hoult), with an unfortunate penchant for Peruvian knit hats and a depressed mother, Fiona (Toni Collette). After Fiona's suicide attempt, young Marcus "adopts" the reluctant Will. The two help each other grow up, making *About a Boy* a coming-of-age story of two "boys," one who's 12 and the other who's 38.

We also loved *High Fidelity,* likewise based on a Nick Hornby novel. Both movies deliver, without too much subtlety, the message: Men Take a *Really* Long Time to Grow Up. Will offers some insight into male narcissism when he describes himself as being "the star of *The Will Show . . . not* an ensemble drama."

Bonding Potential: 6

About a Boy is also about moms, especially single moms. Fiona is lost in her own depression; in her own New Agey, granola way, she's even more selfish than Will. Moms can be unaware of the effect their moods have on their kids, which is why the scenes of Marcus watching his mother's meltdowns are important. Her selfishness is most evident when she comes home after her suicide attempt, her "personal experience," and announces to her son, "I feel better now," oblivious to the impact it had on him. When Will loses it with Fiona and screams, "You daft fucking hippie," we wanted to cheer.

Again, there can never be enough said about the horrors of adolescence. Marcus is such a geek that his only friends, two Pakistani computer nerds, solemnly inform him that they can't hang out with him anymore.

 Hunk Factor: 5

Hugh Grant forgoes his usual bag of tics: stammering, stumbling, bumbling, and blinking. As a result, he's charming and hasn't been this cute in ages.

 Hankie Factor: 6

In one scene, it's hard to know whether to laugh or cry when Fiona breaks down pouring her Ancient Grains cereal.

 Squirming in Your Seat Watching a Sex Scene with Your Mother/Daughter Factor: 0

BEHIND THE SCENES

The directors, Chris and Paul Weitz, whose previous efforts included *American Pie,* are the sons of Susan Kohner, who played Sarah Jane in *Imitation of Life.*

AFTERMATH

The Fox network is considering making *About a Boy* into a sitcom. In February 2003, Hugh Grant won the Empire Award as best British actor of 2003.

Bridget Jones's Diary (2001)

Rated R

Directed by Sharon Maguire

Starring Renée Zellweger, Hugh Grant, Colin Firth, Jim Broadbent, Embeth Davidtz, Gemma Jones, Shirley Henderson, Sally Phillips, James Callis, Paul Brooke

THE PLOT

Bridget Jones's Diary depicts a hilarious year in the life of a British singleton in her thirties who's still searching for Mr. Right. In an effort to take control of her life, Bridget (Renée Zellweger) starts a diary. She vows to find a sensible boyfriend and to stop forming "romantic attach-

216

GENTLEMEN PREFER . . .

1. Any Jackie Chan movie

2. Any James Bond movie

3. Anything with football

4. *Dirty Harry* movies

5. *Lethal Weapon* movies

6. *There's Something About Mary*

7. *Caddyshack*

8. *Dumb and Dumber*

ments to any of the following: alcoholics, workaholics, commitment-phobics, peeping toms, megalomaniacs, emotional nitwits, or perverts."

After her first meeting with Mark Darcy (Colin Firth), in which he refers to her as a "verbally incontinent spinster," she chooses her charismatic boss, Daniel Cleaver (Hugh Grant), "a bona fide sex god," and they embark on an affair rife with misunderstandings and un-spoken feelings. That is, until she asks him if he loves her and the whole relationship heads south. Daniel turns out to be the kind of guy who should wear a flashing red trouble light on his forehead: hand-some, funny, charming, loads of fun, and interested in himself above all else. We've all fallen for him at some point in life, and we know ex-actly what Bridget is going through.

When Bridget runs into the seemingly reserved, repressed, haughty, but eventually smoldering and kind Mark Darcy again, the two of them proceed down the path of unexpressed thoughts and feel-ings. She is still torn between dangerous Daniel and reliable Mark, but her feelings solidify in an instant of recognition.

There are loads of fun characters in *Bridget Jones's Diary*, from her parents (Gemma Jones and Jim Broadbent), to her good-natured chums (Shirley Henderson, Sally Phillips, James Callis), to Daniel's boss, Mr. Fitzherbert (Paul Brooke), whom Bridget calls Mr. Tits Per-vert since he stares freely at her breasts "with no idea who I am or what I do."

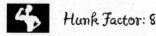 Bonding Potential: 7

Bridget Jones's Diary is about men, self-esteem, and friendship. It's about taking an unconventional path to find out who you are and what you want. Bridget is constantly trying to hide her lack of self-confidence, but she gains a sense of it when someone tells her he likes her *just as she is.*

Hunk Factor: 8

Colin Firth and Hugh Grant—it's hard to argue with that.

Hankie Factor: 0

Squirming in Your Seat Watching a Sex Scene with Your Mother/Daughter Factor: 1

There are a couple of sexual moments, but they are mostly comedic.

BEHIND THE SCENES

Much was made of Renée Zellweger plumping up for the role, but she just looks like a regular girl and not the least bit pudgy. Besides eating more than a carrot stick, Renée actually worked at a British publishing company for a month in preparation for the role. She adopted an alias as well as her posh accent and was apparently not recognized.

AFTERMATH

218

Colin Firth, who played a different Mr. Darcy in the immensely popular BBC/A&E production of *Pride and Prejudice,* is himself a featured character in the book's sequel, *Bridget Jones: The Edge of Reason.* "I was delighted to become a popular-culture reference point. I'm still delighted about it, actually, and I still find it to be weird."

Desert Bloom (1986)
Rated PG

Directed by Eugene Corr
Starring Jon Voight, JoBeth Williams, Annabeth Gish, Ellen Barkin, Allen Garfield

THE PLOT

Rose Chismore (Annabeth Gish) is a sensitive teenager living in 1950s Las Vegas with her mother Lily (JoBeth Williams) and her stepfather Jack (Jon Voight). Jack works in a gas station and suffers from battle fatigue, alcoholism, and depression. He is physically and verbally abusive to Rose. When he learns that the U.S. government is conducting atomic bomb tests in the nearby Nevada desert, Jack starts arming himself for a possible attack. Into their trailer bursts Aunt Starr (Ellen Barkin), a man-crazy glamourpuss waiting for her divorce to come through.

The "bloom" of the title refers to Rose's coming-of-age, her likeness to one of the resilient desert wildflowers, and the ever-present deadly mushroom cloud. Rose learns about life from Aunt Starr and begins to blossom, getting her first kiss from the boy (in the trailer) next door. She blooms after Starr outfits her with a pair of falsies, too!

 Bonding Potential: 5

Girls who have difficulty relating to their stepdads will identify with Rose's plight. We hate how he treated Rose and we really want him to get over himself and the Battle of the Bulge. Yet Rose's mother is so desperate to hold on to her (lousy) marriage and (lousier) husband that she ignores how Jack mistreats the family, particularly her daughter. She speaks in clichés, and her "Every cloud has a silver lining" is especially dumb with the literal and figurative atom bomb cloud lurking over the household. Her denial is detrimental to her family's health. And did we mention that she's a gambling addict?

 Hunk Factor: 2

Jon Voight hasn't been cute since the seventies. But we liked Jay Underwood as Robin, Rose's love interest.

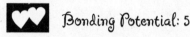 Squirming in Your Seat Watching a Sex Scene with Your Mother/Daughter Factor: 0

BEHIND THE SCENES

Winona Ryder auditioned for the part but lost to Annabeth Gish.

AFTERMATH

Annabeth may have won the part over Winona, but her career never took off. She did an *X-Files* stint on TV.

Say Anything (1989)
Rated PG-13

Directed by Cameron Crowe

Starring John Cusack, Ione Skye, John Mahoney, Lili Taylor, Amy Brooks

THE PLOT

It's high school graduation, and Diane Court (Ione Skye) is the class valedictorian, described as "a brain trapped in the body of a game show hostess." She spent her time in high school with her father (John Mahoney) and at her studies. Her diligence has paid off—she's won a fellowship to study in England. Lloyd Dobler (John Cusack) is smitten with Diane, and when he takes her to a graduation party, it's the first time she's connected with her class. Lloyd's best friends are two girls, Corey (Lili Taylor) and DC (Amy Brooks); his only ambition is to become a champion kickboxer and not "sell anything, buy anything, or process anything." What starts as a friendship between Diane and Lloyd blossoms into something more, despite her disapproving father and their disbelieving classmates. Things get complicated when the IRS starts investigating Dad and his nursing home.

This is as sweet a romance as you're likely to find—about *any* age. Lloyd may be goofy and have limited ambition, but he's a true romantic. He really knows how to love a girl and we understand why Diane falls for him. He sees things more clearly than most guys, and sadly, we're not just talking teenage guys. When he and Diane break up, Lloyd decides to do some male bonding and listens to a bunch of guys mouthing off about women. He offers us this insight into the male psyche when he asks them, "I got a question. If you guys know so much about women, how come you're here at like the Gas 'n' Sip on a Saturday night completely alone drinking beers with no women anywhere?"

Bonding Potential: 7

Diane chose her father in the custody fight because they made a promise they could say anything to each other. Hey, Diane, that's your *mother* you're supposed to make those kinds of pacts with. But we love her anyway: She chose Lloyd, too. Diane's focus is a welcome

221

WHAT WAS SHE THINKING?

1. Lisa Marie Presley and Michael Jackson

2. Kelly LeBrock and Steven Seagal

3. Ashley Judd and Michael Bolton

4. Heather Locklear and Tommy Lee

5. Ava Gardner and Mickey Rooney

6. Mia Farrow and Woody Allen

7. Elizabeth Taylor and Eddie Fisher

8. Claudia Schiffer and David Copperfield

9. Kim Basinger and Prince

10. Beverly D'Angelo and Al Pacino

counterpart to Corey, who is obsessed with her ex-boyfriend Joe. In a true get-a-life moment, we find out that Corey wrote sixty-three songs about Joe. In one year.

 Hunk Factor: 9

John Cusack is the most offbeat hottie of our time. We defy you to resist him.

 Hankie Factor: 0

Squirming in Your Seat Watching a Sex Scene with Your Mother/Daughter Factor: 0

222 BEHIND THE SCENES

The most famous scene in the movie is when Lloyd stands outside Diane's house, serenading her with a boom box playing their song, "In Your Eyes." Peter Gabriel wrote this song for Rosanna Arquette.

AFTERMATH

While John Cusack went on to be a big star, alas, the same is not true of Ione Skye. She is all too visible on a number of Internet porn sites.

School Ties (1992)

Rated PG-13

el

Matt Damon, Chris O'Donnell, Ben Affleck, Cole Hauser,
Randall Batinkoff, Amy Locane

rep school recruits David Greene (Brendan
Jewish high school senior, for their football
nti-Semitism is so commonplace that David
n from his classmates. He notices how his
amon), Chris (Chris O'Donnell), Van (Ran-
ndrew Lowery) are under constant pres-
perform, get into Ivy League colleges, and
ons. Despite his outsider status, David be-
lose friendship with Charlie, though the re-
David overtakes him on the football team
Amy Locane). When his secret is revealed,
int anti-Semitism, dropped by his girlfriend,
ating on an exam.

he casual and accepted anti-Semitism of some
ed him down to twenty dollars," says one char-
n the shower:

> *Waist-Up Guy 1:* I wouldn't go to Harvard if
> you paid me—all those Jews
> and communists.
> *Waist-Up Guy 2:* Yeah, and that's just the faculty!

On
Guys litical level, it reveals something really important:
petitiv high school guys, can be just as bitchy, jealous, com-
they're e, and mean-spirited as high school girls (except
nodest in the shower).

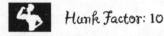 Bonding Potential: 7

Most everybody feels like an outsider in high school, but Davi[d] [re]ally is, which is why his journey is so moving. On a lighter [note,] *School Ties* offers a *Football for Dummies* lesson. The gam[e se]quences are so easy to follow that even diehard football phobic[s can] follow what's going on.

 Hunk Factor: 10

Are you kidding? Fraser, Damon, O'Donnell, Hauser, Afflec[k are] all in various states of undress, including some (literally) [steamy] shower scenes.

 Hankie Factor: 2

Squirming in Your Seat Watching a Sex Scene with [Your] Mother/Daughter Factor: 0

BEHIND THE SCENES

Brendan Fraser's character is named David Greene, the sa[me] as a character in *Gentlemen's Agreement,* Hollywood's fi[rst film] about anti-Semitism. Matt Damon said the director kept [telling the] cast they were going to be the "next brat pack."

AFTERMATH

School Ties draws from the life of its writer, TV producer [Dick Wolf,] who attended prep school at Andover. Wolf, who seems t[o have fond] memories of his alma mater, went on to produce *Law and* [Order.]

The Stepford Wives (1975)
Rated PG

Directed by Bryan Forbes

Starring Katharine Ross, Paula Prentiss, Peter Masterson, Nanette Newman, Tina Louise

THE PLOT

Something's rotten in the town of Stepford. The wives, apron-wearing automatons, are all so devoted to housework that they would make Martha Stewart look like Pig Pen. Their husbands congregate nightly at the local men's association, where together they seem to be up to who knows what. Joanna and Walter Eberheart (Katharine Ross and Peter Masterson), with their two daughters, are recent transplants from New York City, and though Walter seems enamored of suburban living, Joanna, an avid photographer, isn't so thrilled about leaving the city behind. She can't seem to share her husband's infatuation with casserole dinners, quiet nights, and neighborhood pool parties soggy with politesse. And she just can't shake the feeling that there is something wrong with all these women, who rave about cleaning products like paid spokespeople and dress like Donna Reed. Only her new best friend, Bobbie (Paula Prentiss), also a recent arrival, shares her suspicions, and together they set out to uncover the secret behind their neighbors' seemingly perfect lives.

The Stepford Wives is a masterpiece of black comedy and slow-building horror, all the more creepy and unnerving for taking place mostly in beautifully appointed houses and bright, sunny backyards. Katharine Ross (star of *The Graduate* and *Butch Cassidy and the Sundance Kid*) gives an understated and affecting performance as an alienated woman who watches, terrified, as all the wives around her are transformed into mindless Holly Homemakers.

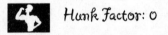 Bonding Potential: 7

The Stepford Wives is to women's lib what *Invasion of the Body Snatchers* was to Communism. Made in the mid-1970s, the movie imagines a particularly nightmarish reaction by a group of male suburbanites to the gains made by feminism in the previous decade. Rather than love the women they married, these ruthless chauvinists set out to engineer for themselves perfect wives, always cleaning, always baking, always commending them on their performance in bed.

This movie can serve as an interesting springboard for mother-daughter discussions about women's role in society, then and now. The husbands view women as service providers and nothing more; their individual personality traits—Joanna's artistic ambitions, Bobbie's moxie—are considered impediments to the performance of their household functions. And so they are reduced to obedient, industrious mannequins. The film is a sci-fi allegory as much as it is a horror film, and it spoofs what Maureen Dowd once called the male fear of female assertion that was very much still a reality when the film was made. Science, much to the chagrin of men everywhere, hasn't yet found a way to turn women into femmebots, but women still struggle to find some balance between work and home, to juggle the demands of being mothers, wives, and individuals.

 Hunk Factor: 0

You'll know something strange must be afoot when all these ugly middle-aged men have such gorgeous wives.

Hankie Factor: 6

Stepford, the movie and the town, slowly closes around Joanna like a trap. Though you may not cry, she certainly does, desperate, afraid, fearing for her own sanity and safety. Be prepared for an ending that is at once funny, sad, and altogether unsettling.

Squirming in Your Seat Watching a Sex Scene with Your
Mother/Daughter Factor: 0

It's clear that these sexy, servile zombies are devoted to satisfying *all* their husbands' needs. Thank goodness we don't have to see any of it. We just can't stress it enough: These guys are stinkers.

BEHIND THE SCENES

Look out for then 9-year-old Mary Stuart Masterson in her screen debut, playing daughter to her real-life dad, Peter.

AFTERMATH

The Stepford Wives was remade in 2003 into a movie starring Nicole Kidman, Matthew Broderick, Bette Midler, and Christopher Walken.

227

What's Eating Gilbert Grape? (1993)
Rated PG-13

Directed by Lasse Hallström

Starring Johnny Depp, Leonardo DiCaprio, Juliette Lewis, Mary Steenburgen, Darlene Cates, Laura Harrington, Mary Kate Schellhardt

THE PLOT

Gilbert Grape (Johnny Depp) lives in Endora, a small town in Iowa (population 1,091). He's the father figure of an unusual family that includes two sisters (Laura Harrington, Mary Kate Schellhardt), a severely retarded 18-year-old brother Arnie (Leonardo DiCaprio), and last, but certainly not least, his 500-pound mother (Darlene Cates). Mom hasn't left the house in seven years; in fact she never leaves the couch, taking her meals and sleeping there. Arnie demands much of Gilbert's time, especially since he keeps climbing the town's water tower, an event that attracts the police and most of the town. In addition to taking care of Arnie, Gilbert works at the local grocery store. He's carrying on an affair with one of the customers, a married housewife (Mary Steenburgen), and theirs is a dalliance that seems like just another one of his responsibilities. When Becky (Juliette Lewis) comes to town in her RV, she and

TRANSCENDING
THE GENERATIONS:
HUNKS AND HOTTIES

1. Will Smith, *Bad Boys*

2. Adrian Brody, *The Pianist*

3. Viggo Mortensen, *Lord of the Rings*

4. Robert Downey Jr., *Chaplin*

5. Clive Owen, *Croupier*

6. Brad Pitt, *Legends of the Fall*

7. Keanu Reeves, *A Walk in the Clouds*

8. Russell Crowe, *Gladiator*

9. Liam Neeson, *Michael Collins*

10. Benjamin Bratt, *Piñero*

11. Javier Bardem, *Before Night Falls*

12. Dennis Haysbert, *Love Field*

13. Taye Diggs, *How Stella Got Her Groove Back*

14. Benicio Del Toro, *Traffic*

Gilbert are attracted to each other. In the errant Becky, Gilbert sees the freedom he has never had, and their blossoming romance makes it difficult for Gilbert to remain such a dutiful son and brother.

The Grape family could easily be considered a bunch of freaks, but the film portrays them with warmth and respect. They accept themselves, they accept their mother, they accept Arnie, and when Arnie turns 18, half the town shows up for his birthday party. Still, Mama is a local curiosity, and at one point she's forced to acknowledge "what a burden [she's] been." But when she finally leaves her couch, heads downtown to rescue Arnie from one of his many misadventures, and shouts at the sheriff, "Give me my son!" she earns the respect and admiration of everyone in the town and in the audience.

 ### Bonding Potential: 6

Look how protective the Grape kids are of Mama. Mama, formerly "the most beautiful woman in Endora," now has the kitchen table brought over to her for her many, many fried meals. Her kids love and nurture her, and the scene where Gilbert brings Becky home to meet her is the most important moment in the movie. When Gilbert is asked what he wishes for, he says, "I wish my mother would take aerobic classes." Let's hope he doesn't mean high-impact classes, however, since when Mama stamps her foot, the entire foundation of the house starts shifting.

Hunk Factor: 10

Johnny Depp alone earns this movie a 10 rating. Leonardo isn't exactly hunk material here, but his legions of fans shouldn't miss this movie, because Arnie is one of his best performances, and even earned him an Academy Award nomination for best supporting actor.

Hankie Factor: 5

Needed for the scene when Mama looks at Gilbert:

Mama: You're my knight in shimmering armor. Did you know
　　　that?

Gilbert: I think you mean shining.

Mama: No, shimmering. You shimmer, and you glow.

 Squirming in Your Seat Watching a Sex Scene with Your
Mother/Daughter Factor: 0

BEHIND THE SCENES

The filmmakers discovered Darlene Cates, a nonprofessional from
Texas, when she appeared on the *Sally Jesse Raphael Show.*

AFTERMATH

The following year, Depp, who played such a sober, selfless character
in *Grape,* trashed his suite at New York's trendy Mark Hotel, causing
$10,000 worth of damage. Johnny claimed a cockroach was trying to
attack him. Another aftereffect was the release of the porno movie
Who's Eating Gilbert Grape?

230

OLDER TEENS ONLY

The Good Girl (2002)
Rated R

Directed by Miguel Arteta

Starring Jennifer Aniston, Jake Gyllenhaal, John C. Reilly, Zooey Deschanel, Tim Blake
　　Nelson

THE PLOT

At 30, Justine (Jennifer Aniston) works at the Retail Rodeo in a small
Texas town. She's married to a housepainter, Phil (John C. Reilly), who

likes to smoke pot and watch cartoons with his pal, Bubba (Tim Blake Nelson). Justine is depressed and feels as if her life is over. The only break from the tedium at the Retail Rodeo is when Cheryl (Zooey Deschanel) inserts obscenities into the PA system. But then Justine strikes up a friendship with the new cashier, Holden (Jake Gyllenhaal), who has just gotten kicked out of college for drinking. Right away Justine tells Holden, "I saw in your eyes that you hate the world," she says. "I hate it, too." The two start an affair, but it doesn't take Justine a long time to figure out that her young lover is needy and unstable.

Wow, just when we thought *our* life was boring, we meet Justine. "As a girl," she tells us, "you see the world as a giant candy store filled with sweet candy and such." So far we agree with that, but then she adds, "When you get older, you realize you're locked up in a prison with no way out." Why doesn't she take night school classes? Or Zoloft?

 Bonding Potential: 6

It's a good thing *The Good Girl* is so funny, because Justine is really depressed. Part of her malaise is the men in her life. Her husband, good-natured but not too bright, is too much of a stoner to keep her respect. "He's a pig, he talks, but he doesn't think." His pal and fellow buffoon, Bubba, turns out to be harboring a weird, deep secret. The security guard at the Retail Rodeo is a Bible-thumping creep.

Although Justine thinks Holden could be her salvation, he turns out to be self-destructive and dangerous, and actually named Tom. It's hard to stay the good girl with these kinds of guys around. Justine does find a way out, and hard as it is to believe, the movie winds up being (oddly) uplifting.

 Hunk Factor: 3ish

There are some out there who find Jake Gyllenhaal appealing.

Hankie Factor: 0

231

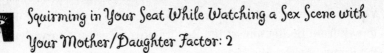

There are some sex scenes, but *Friends* fans looking to see more of Jennifer will be disappointed.

BEHIND THE SCENES

In an interview about *The Good Girl,* Miguel Arteta said, "If you conform, it's like a life sentence. But if you rebel, you don't have a place in society." He sounds like Justine—could he be depressed, too?

AFTERMATH

In *The Good Girl,* Jennifer Aniston plays a character sleepwalking through life. In real life, she literally is a sleepwalker. After she made this movie, she walked in her sleep, went out of her house, and set off the security system.

Rosemary's Baby (1968)

Rated R

Directed by Roman Polanski
Starring Mia Farrow, John Cassavetes, Ruth Gordon, Sidney Blackmer, Maurice Evans

THE PLOT

It's October 1965, the pope is visiting New York, and Rosemary (Mia Farrow) is looking for an apartment with Guy (John Cassavetes), her actor-husband. They decide on a place in a building called the Bramford, even though a family friend, Hutch (Maurice Evans), has warned them against it, telling them the building has a dark and bizarre history. Once they move in, they meet their next-door neighbors, an elderly couple named Minnie and Roman Castavet (Ruth Gordon and Sidney Blackmer). Rosemary is puzzled by her husband's sudden attachment to the oldsters, particularly since she finds them so overbearing. After a "nightmare" in which she dreams she was raped, Rosemary finds out that she's going to have a baby. She's delighted, but the pregnancy soon proves to be difficult and painful. While Guy's acting career is suddenly taking off, he becomes a distant husband, even avoiding eye contact with Rosemary.

This is a horror movie with little blood and no gore. One of its scariest moments is simple kitchen stuff—Rosemary is eating raw liver and catches her reflection in the toaster. She doesn't know what's happening to her and *really* doesn't know her husband—that makes for true terror. *Rosemary's Baby* raises some real questions about bad versus good, the price of ambition, the sometime banal face of evil, and mother love.

 Bonding Potential: 7

Rosemary worships her husband (never a good thing) and is content to live in the reflected glory of his acting career. Hey, Ro—stop reciting his résumé! But she doesn't understand his self-obsession, his ambition, or his fascination with their nosy neighbors. Didn't her mother tell her never to marry an actor? Guy is even worse than the tall, dark, and well . . . strange stranger she meets one night across a crowded coven.

Another important lesson to be learned from *Rosemary's Baby*: Don't go to dismissive male obstetricians. Rosemary, passive throughout the movie, finally becomes defiant, thanks to an infusion of mom power, when she realizes she must save her baby.

 Hankie Factor: 0

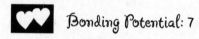 Squirming in Your Seat Watching a Sex Scene with Your Mother/Daughter Factor: 0

BEHIND THE SCENES

During filming, Mia Farrow was devastated when her husband, Frank Sinatra, served her with divorce papers. She recovered, however, when she saw rushes of the film. Director Roman Polanski's wife, Sharon Tate, is said to be in the party scene, though we couldn't spot her (freeze-framed and everything). The following year, 1969, Sharon was murdered in her home by members of the Manson Family, a Southern California cult dedicated to a creepy failed musician, Charles Manson. She was pregnant at the time.

AFTERMATH

Anton Sander LaVey, founder of the Church of Satan, was rumored to be an adviser on the film. Before she discovered Charles Manson, Susan Atkins—the cult member who actually killed Sharon Tate—was a follower of LaVey's. Sharon's murder was part of the Family's death spree called "Helter Skelter," a name they borrowed from a Beatle song. The opening segment of *Rosemary's Baby* was filmed at the entrance of the Dakota apartment building, the very spot where Beatle John Lennon was murdered in 1980.

234

Saturday Night Fever (1977)
Rated R

Directed by John Badham
Starring John Travolta, Karen Lynn Gorney, Barry Miller, Joseph Cali, Paul Pape, Donna
    Pescow

THE PLOT

This is a story of breaking away, of cutting loose from the philosophical and material limitations offered by a working-class Italian Catholic family in Bay Ridge, Brooklyn. By day, 19-year-old Tony Manero (John Travolta) works at a hardware and paint store. By night, he is the dance king at 2001 Odyssey Disco. His parents' proudest achievement is having a son, Tony's brother Frank, who is a priest. At the other end of the spectrum is having a son Tony, who is a dancer. Tony is a complex character, simultaneously angry and vulnerable—his vulnerability makes us able to empathize with such a dark, sexist character. He is becoming an adult and forming an independent identity as he sees himself and his buddies doing things that no longer feel right to him. Tony has a faint ache of wanting more, but that ache hasn't articulated itself clearly in his mind yet. In the disco, Tony's effortlessly graceful dancing is a gift; he's adored by everyone, but by no one as much as Annette (Donna Pescow), who makes one bad choice after another in an effort to attract him. He runs with a posse of Bay Ridge boys including Bobby C. (Barry Miller), Joey (Joseph Cali), and Double J (Paul Pape) who are equally racist, sexist, and foul-mouthed, but this is Tony's story—told from his perspective and with him in nearly every scene. Tony is drawn to the striving, name-dropping Stephanie (Karen Lynn Gorney), who tells him that he's a cliché. "You're nowhere on your way to no place." He feels the pull to get out, but he is too frightened and she, with her secretarial job in the city, represents sophistication to him.

This movie holds up incredibly well. *Saturday Night Fever* is the quintessential movie of the disco era: sex, drugs, tight polyester clothing, and the Hustle. Time has faded the hard edges, and instead of remembering the difficult, challenging images, we are left with those of Tony strutting down the street and dancing to the Bee Gees in his beautiful white suit.

 Bonding Potential: 8

This is a look into a subculture of men who have no idea of how to treat women. After dinner one evening, Tony is helping clear the table and his father tells him to stop because that is girl's work. His parents' traditional aspirations inform Tony's idea of himself. He treats women as objects until his affection forces him to see at least one woman as a person.

At 23, Travolta played 19. He was in the prime of his prime. There are many shots of him moving and grooving on the dance floor (which are a treat), but there are also several shots of him in his skivvies in his own room. Do we want to mother him or sleep with him? Yikes!

235

Hunk Factor: 10

John Travolta is completely irresistible as he dances in his tight, high-waisted poly pants and patterned poly shirt. He looks even yummier showing off his perfect fitness when clad only in briefs. Is there anyone who didn't want to put on a short poly dress with stacked heels and get out on the dance floor with him?

 Hankie Factor: 2

Maybe in the last ten minutes.

Squirming in Your Seat Watching a Sex Scene with Your Mother/Daughter Factor: 9

There are some very rough scenes in the backseat of the car that you might not want to share with your mother/daughter. Please note that there is a PG-13 version available.

BEHIND THE SCENES

This was one of the many big and memorable movies made by the late great cinematographer Ralf Bode. Its importance and resonance is underscored by the fact that, over a quarter century after it was made, it is still the main movie he is known for. After Bode used star filters in this movie, they turned up everywhere.

During the editing process, John Travolta, then only 23, was given the final cut of his dance solo. Travolta originally wanted his disco suit to be black until it was pointed out that in the darkened disco, a black suit would make him disappear. The white suit, bought off the rack in a store, is now in the Smithsonian.

AFTERMATH

Norman Wexler's screenplay was adapted from the "nonfiction" *New York* magazine article written by Nik Cohn. Years later, Cohn admitted that the story, supposedly a fact-based account detailing the lives of Brooklyn teenagers in the early days of the disco craze, was a complete fabrication.

P.S. Richard Gere practically owes his film career to Travolta. Travolta turned down the leads for *Days of Heaven, American Gigolo, An Officer and a Gentleman,* and finally, *Chicago.*

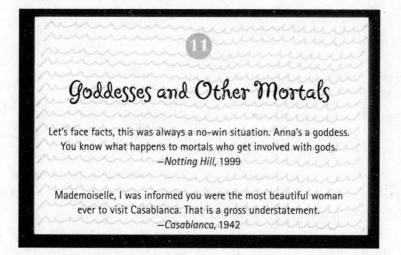

11

Goddesses and Other Mortals

Let's face facts, this was always a no-win situation. Anna's a goddess.
You know what happens to mortals who get involved with gods.
—*Notting Hill,* 1999

Mademoiselle, I was informed you were the most beautiful woman
ever to visit Casablanca. That is a gross understatement.
—*Casablanca,* 1942

The word *goddess* is tossed around a lot these days, particularly in posturing New Age circles. In our opinion, however,
the only true goddesses were those who radiantly looked down
on us from the silver screen. These dames owned their films,
dominating every scene they were in and staying with you long
after the credits have rolled. Of course, they all had messed-up
personal lives the likes of which Winona "Sticky Fingers" Ryder
has never seen, but this only serves to remind us that they were
in fact from this galaxy and all too human. Watching one of
these movies when you're feeling less than luminous will help
you rediscover your inner deity, and all girls need that once in a
while.

All About Eve (1950)

Rated PG

Directed by Joseph L. Mankiewicz

Starring Bette Davis, Anne Baxter, Celeste Holm, George Sanders, Gary Merrill,

Marilyn Monroe, Thelma Ritter, Hugh Marlowe

THE PLOT

Aging (by the standards of 1950, anyhow) Broadway diva Margo
Channing (Bette Davis) takes pity on her most devoted fan, "the lost
lamb" Eve Harrington (Anne Baxter). Margo hires Eve as her assistant but soon realizes that the younger woman is plotting to take over
her career, her boyfriend (Gary Merrill), her friends (Celeste Holm,
Thelma Ritter, Hugh Marlowe), and in fact her entire life.

240

Today, more than fifty years after its release, *All About Eve* is called
"The Bitchiest Movie Ever Made." It was far ahead of its time in terms
of plot and dialogue, and Margo's great line "Fasten your seat belt. It's
going to be a bumpy night" has provided fodder for generations of
drag queens.

Bonding Potential: 5

Young women should realize that there was a time, and *not* a long,
long time ago, in this very galaxy, that women were considered old at
40. Margo gets a snootful and declares, "I am not twentyish. I am not
thirtyish. Three months ago I was forty years old. Forty. Four-oh.
That slipped out. I hadn't quite made up my mind to admit it. Now I
feel as though I've suddenly taken all my clothes off."

Okay, so there are no mothers in this movie and Eve is truly the
Anti-Sister, but there are great women characters and dynamics.
Margo is a woman with—pardon the expression—balls. Still, at the
core, she is a loving, vulnerable artist. Her best girlfriend Karen (Celeste Holm) finally helps her battle Eve, while Margo's maid, Birdie

(Thelma Ritter), is the first to enlighten Margo about Eve: "She reminds me of an agent with one client."

![icon] **Hunk Factor: 2**

While there's not much in terms of hunkitude, Gary Merrill had what used to be called animal magnetism. And if your tastes run to cads of ambiguous sexuality, there's always George Sanders.

![icon] **Hankie Factor: 0**

Too bitchy to be sad.

![icon] **Squirming in Your Seat Watching a Sex Scene with Your Mother/Daughter Factor: 0**

241

BEHIND THE SCENES

Bette Davis and Gary Merrill fell in love during *All About Eve* and married soon afterwards. Their all-night drinking (and other stuff) caused them to show up late and hung over for shooting. Celeste Holm recalled her first day on the set: She greeted Bette with "Good morning" to which Bette replied, "Oh shit, good manners." They never spoke again. In *All About All About Eve*, Sam Staggs relates that newcomer Marilyn Monroe, who played a showgirl sleeping her way to the top, was doing exactly that during the filming.

AFTERMATH

All About Eve was the most nominated movie until *Titanic*. In 1983, there was lots of clucking about life imitating art when Anne Baxter replaced Bette Davis in the TV series *Hotel* after Davis became ill. Fifty years after Miss Bette Davis first appeared on the screen, the song "Bette Davis Eyes" became one of the big hits of 1981, a testament to her enduring star power.

The Barefoot Contessa (1954)

Not rated

Directed by Joseph L. Mankiewicz

Starring Ava Gardner, Humphrey Bogart, Edmond O'Brien, Rossano Brazzi, Warren Stevens, Elizabeth Sellars

THE PLOT

Maria Vargas (Ava Gardner), a flamenco dancer, is discovered in a small town in Spain by wannabe film producer Kirk Edwards (Warren Stevens), sweaty publicist Oscar Muldoon (Edmond O'Brien), and wise but weary director Harry Dawes (Humphrey Bogart). At first Maria tells the crowd to get lost, but Harry, whom she instantly trusts, convinces her to take a screen test. The test is a smash and she becomes a big movie star. Maria finds Hollywood phony and filled with phonies, the only exceptions being Harry and his new fiancée, Jerry (Elizabeth Sellars). So Maria takes off to Europe, where she finds the Eurotrash and deposed royalty as distasteful as the Hollywood crowd *until* she meets a handsome nobleman with an impressive moniker, Count Vincenzo Torlato-Favrini (Rossano Brazzi). The two fall madly in love and marry, though Maria's honeymoon proves to be a bit of a letdown.

Some narrow-minded people think this is a bad movie. We don't agree, but if it is a bad movie, it's a *good* bad movie. Besides, here's a chance to watch one of the greatest goddesses in the movies, Ava Gardner. Gorgeous and husky-voiced, she does a mean flamenco. She even has a haircut that on anyone else would be downright butch. The 1954 ads billed her as "The world's most beautiful animal!" Try getting away with that these days . . .

Bonding Potential: 6

Yes, a campy movie about a movie star who hates shoes—"I feel afraid in shoes and I feel safe with my feet in the dirt"—is bonding! Grab the popcorn and watch this last gasp of Hollywood glamour (with apologies to Miss Catherine Zeta-Jones) in all its Technicolor glory.

Oddly, *The Barefoot Contessa* makes an (unintentional) case for premarital sex: Maria holds out until her honeymoon with the count, and then our girl gets a *really* nasty surprise. They didn't spell it out for you in 1954, but here's a hint—he has lost something in the war.

 Hunk Factor: 0

 Hankie Factor: 0

Squirming in Your Seat Watching a Sex Scene with Your Mother/Daughter Factor: 0

BEHIND THE SCENES

The movie was loosely based on the life of another glam movie star, Rita Hayworth, who was unhappily married to an international play-boy. The character of Kirk Edwards is based on eccentric billionaire Howard Hughes. In real life Hughes pursued Ava Gardner, and once during a fight, she hit him over the head with an ashtray and knocked him out cold.

AFTERMATH

Ava Gardner, like Maria Vargas, had little use for Hollywood, finding it corrupt and boring. After finishing *The Barefoot Contessa,* she made her permanent home in Maria's native Spain.

Breakfast at Tiffany's (1961)

Not rated

Directed by Blake Edwards

Starring Audrey Hepburn, George Peppard, Buddy Ebsen, Patricia Neal, Mickey
  Rooney

THE PLOT

Holly Golightly (Audrey Hepburn) is a sophisticated New Yorker who
throws great parties, wears designer clothes, and uses a ten-inch cigarette holder. Go, Holly! As one character describes her, "She's a
phony. But a real phony." She's unemployed and her revenue source
is suspect, but it seems that she somehow manages to live off men.
Her new neighbor is writer/quasi-gigolo Paul (George Peppard). Paul
is being kept by a rich married lady (Patricia Neal) who wears outfits
similar to Snow White's stepmother. It's inconvenient, but Paul and
Holly start falling for each other. Then Holly's cracker past, in the
form of Doc Golightly (Buddy Ebsen), catches up with her.

Audrey Hepburn is transcendent and makes *Breakfast at Tiffany's*
a classic. The movie even popped up in a *Seinfeld* episode: George
hadn't read his book club's selection, *Breakfast at Tiffany's*, the
novella by Truman Capote. He decided to rent the movie instead, but
when the video store told him it was out, George showed up at the
home of the family that rented it, and they all sat on the couch and
watched *Breakfast at Tiffany's* together.

♥ *Bonding Potential: 9*

Mothers and daughters will both fall under Holly's spell. Hey, who
wouldn't love a girl who says, "Cross my heart and kiss my elbow," or
"I've got to do something about the way I look. I mean, a girl just can't
go to Sing Sing with a green face." Only the crankiest viewer might
mention that Holly is a party girl and a nutty male dependent, and

never goes to the gym, either. But we don't care. Audrey Hepburn set the standard for sophistication, class, and style for generations, and so far no one has taken her place. (Sorry, Julia.)

 Hunk Factor: 4

George Peppard is definitely handsome, but doughy in a way that is forbidden to modern buff hunks.

WHEN YOU'RE SICK IN BED (OR GUILTY PLEASURES)

1. *Invisible Child* (or anything else on Lifetime)
2. *Karate Kid*
3. Any Shirley Temple movie
4. *Grease*
5. *An Affair to Remember*
6. *A Walk to Remember*
7. *How to Marry a Millionaire*
8. *Babe*
9. *When Harry Met Sally . . .*
10. *A Knight's Tale*
11. *The Importance of Being Earnest* (Colin Firth version)

245

Hankie Factor: 3

Somehow it was the cat that got us.

Squirming in Your Seat Watching a Sex Scene with Your Mother/Daughter Factor: 6

It's not a sex scene, but every discussion of *Breakfast at Tiffany's* must include a big warning about the offensive, racist performance

MORE HUNKS

They were beautiful...

1. Robert De Niro in *Godfather II*

2. Peter O'Toole in *Lawrence of Arabia*

3. Marlon Brando in *On the Waterfront*

4. Warren Beatty in *Bonnie and Clyde*

5. Steve McQueen in *Bullitt*

6. Richard Gere in *Days of Heaven*

7. Humphrey Bogart in *Casablanca*

8. Robert Redford in *The Sting*

9. Paul Newman in *Hud*

10. Cary Grant in *Notorious*

Mickey Rooney gives as the Mr. Yunioshi, the Japanese man who lives upstairs. It wasn't funny even in 1961 and is a major squirm factor today.

BEHIND THE SCENES

Svelte Audrey had a baby just three months before shooting. Author Truman Capote campaigned (and lost) for Marilyn Monroe to play Holly.

AFTERMATH

George Peppard started to look like Mickey Rooney.

Double Indemnity (1944)
Not rated

Directed by Billy Wilder
Starring Barbara Stanwyck, Fred MacMurray, Edward G. Robinson, Tom Powers, Jean
    Heather

THE PLOT

Walter Neff (Fred MacMurray), a salesman for the Pacific All-Risk Insurance Company, stops by the home of Phyllis Dietrichson (Barbara Stanwyck) to check on an auto insurance policy owned by her husband (Tom Powers). It's lust at first sight, as evidenced by the snappy lines of dialogue Walter and Phyllis toss back and forth.

She: I wonder if I know what you mean.
He: I wonder if you wonder.

Their talk of auto insurance turns into accident insurance, and pretty soon the steamy couple are plotting murder. They bump off hubby, making it look like an accident so Phyllis can collect on the

MORE HUNKS

Sam Shepard in . . .

1. *Voyager*

2. *Raggedy Man*

3. *Days of Heaven*

4. *Frances*

5. *Baby Boom*

248

double indemnity insurance policy. After the murder, Walter's coworker and mentor, Keyes (Edward G. Robinson), smells a rat in the Dietrichson insurance case. Keyes shares his suspicions with Walter. To make matters worse, Phyllis is beginning to give Walter the brush-off. The bloom is off the romance and Walter realizes Phyllis is one tough cookie.

Film noir meets pulp fiction meets double entendre in *Double Indemnity*. One might wonder why a movie about an icy murderess wearing a cheesy blonde wig belongs in a compendium of mother-daughter movies. The answer is Barbara Stanwyck as Phyllis Dietrichson. Okay, so Phyllis isn't exactly a role model, but she does get off some of the best dame dialogue in the history of the movies:

"I thought you were smarter than the rest, Walter. But I was wrong. You're not smarter, just a little taller."

"I hope I've got my face on straight."

"I'm rotten to the heart."

Bonding Potential: 6

Femme fatales have fallen out of fashion, so it's a learning experience to watch Phyllis Dietrichson descend a staircase, show off her ankle, and generally disperse pheromones around the screen. She plans murder and serves iced tea with the same affect—none. Walter never had a chance.

 Hunk Factor: 0

Hankie Factor: 0

Squirming in Your Seat Watching a Sex Scene with Your Mother/Daughter Factor: 0

BEHIND THE SCENES

Double Indemnity was based on the true story of housewife Ruth Snyder, who along with her corset salesman boyfriend knocked off her husband. Raymond Chandler cowrote the screenplay and created the classic dialogue even though he was totally drunk the whole time. Midway through the film, director Wilder realized how silly Barbara's wig looked, but by then it was too late. Later he claimed the cheap wig was intentional.

AFTERMATH

Barbara's sexuality has long been the subject of rumors. She was reported to be a member of Hollywood's "sewing circle" (translation: lesbians), and her marriage to Robert Taylor has been called a "lavender" one.

P.S. The 1981 movie *Body Heat* ripped off *Double Indemnity* and never gave any credit to the original.

Gentlemen Prefer Blondes (1953)

Not rated

Directed by Howard Hawks

Starring Marilyn Monroe, Jane Russell, Charles Coburn, Tommy Noonan, Elliott Reid

THE PLOT

Showgirls and fortune hunters Lorelei Lee (Marilyn Monroe) and Dorothy Shaw (Jane Russell) take a luxury liner to Europe. Lorelei leaves behind her rich but nerdy boyfriend (Tommy Noonan); on the boat, she befriends Sir Francis Beekman (Charles Coburn) upon learning the old goat owns a diamond mine. Dorothy dances around with some Olympic swimmers but finds herself falling for Ernie Malone (Elliott Reid). Little does she know that Ernie is a private eye, trying to get the goods on her bestest girlfriend, Lorelei.

Even today, Marilyn's image is everywhere. She's the subject of books, songs, movies, countless Web sites, and even beach towels. Attention spans may be getting smaller, but forty years after her death, Marilyn's cult continues to grow. How can we explain this phenomenon to our daughters and even to ourselves? Simple. Just rent *Gentlemen Prefer Blondes*.

 Bonding Potential: 8

For some reason, watching Marilyn sing "Diamonds Are a Girl's Best Friend" is an incredible bonding experience. It's also a *mandatory* experience for daughters and moms if their only exposure to Marilyn is Madonna's cheesy impersonation. Marilyn succeeds in making us love Lorelei despite her un-PC outlook on love—"It's just as easy to fall in love with a rich man as a poor man"—and her reasons for playing dumb: "I can be smart when it's important, but men don't like it."

Hunk Factor: 0

Hankie Factor: 0

The only way you would need a hankie is if you listen to Elton John's song about Marilyn, "Candle in the Wind," after watching the movie.

Squirming in Your Seat Watching a Sex Scene with Your Mother/Daughter Factor: 0

Although there are plenty of unintentional laughs when Jane makes lecherous overtures toward the male chorus playing Olympic swimmers.

BEHIND THE SCENES

In 1953, Marilyn made this movie and posed in the first issue of a brand-new magazine, *Playboy*. Her favorite drink, coincidentally, was Dom Pérignon 1953.

AFTERMATH

Marilyn became the biggest movie star of all time. Jane Russell (and no, she's not a male transvestite) emerged as simply someone who was in a Marilyn Monroe movie and later hawked brassieres and the Bible. Recently she gave an interview to *The Enquirer* where she claimed, "I say I'm a mean-spirited right-wing conservative Christian bigot!" Jane, nobody cares.

Gone With the Wind (1939)

Rated G

Directed by Victor Fleming

Starring Vivien Leigh, Clark Gable, Olivia de Havilland, Leslie Howard, Hattie
McDaniel

THE PLOT

At the advent of the Civil War, beautiful Southern belle Scarlett O'Hara
(Vivien Leigh) realizes the war is already cramping her social life.
Scarlett pursues her next-door neighbor Ashley Wilkes (Leslie
Howard), who marries the saintly Melanie (Olivia de Havilland) while
Scarlett herself is being pursued by Rhett Butler (Clark Gable), a man
with a past. The war begins in earnest, and Scarlett, in rapid succes-
sion, finds herself married, widowed, motherless, poor, and the head
of a starving household. During Reconstruction, she moves to Atlanta
and becomes a ruthless businesswoman. Throughout it all, Scarlett
still pines after her first love, Ashley, even after she marries Rhett and
the two have a child. Throughout all her adventures, Mammy (Hattie
McDaniel) watches over her charge, Scarlett, with love, amazement,
and very often, disgust.

Generations of women have loved *Gone With the Wind* and Scarlett
O'Hara, despite some of her appalling personality traits. While it may
be difficult for today's young women to get past the inherent racism
and blithe treatment of slavery in the film, it's important to place its
racial insensitivity within the context of its time. When Hattie Mc-
Daniel won the Oscar for her portrayal of the strong, wise Mammy, it
was the first time an African-American had been so honored.

Some years ago, the American Film Institute named *Gone With the
Wind* as one of the hundred best movies of all time. It should be
pointed out that *Gone With the Wind* was the *only* one in the top five
with a female protagonist.

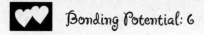 **Bonding Potential: 6**

This has been a seminal moviegoing experience for over sixty years, due in no small part to the magnificent performance of Vivien Leigh. She even looks beautiful in the raggedy dress she wears through a third of the movie. After we saw this—on the big screen, natch—we couldn't help but wonder if Scarlett might have made better choices if only she'd had a few girlfriends to confer with. Scarlett does, however, have a mother, and unfortunately for her, she's a perfect one. She wants to be as serene as Mom, which of course she never is. Good for us, however, because then *GWTW* would have been a snore instead of a four-hour romantic blockbuster.

 Hunk Factor: 8

One of the reasons the movie has held up so well is that Clark Gable is a hunk for the ages. Some viewers also swoon over Leslie Howard as Ashley Wilkes.

253

 Hankie Factor: 10

None needed until the second half, and then bring on the Kleenex.

 Squirming in Your Seat Watching a Sex Scene with Your Mother/Daughter Factor: 0

BEHIND THE SCENES

Gone With the Wind is part of Hollywood lore, generating countless books and a two-hour documentary. It was the brainchild of its producer, David O. Selznick, one of the first people in showbiz to recognize the power of buzz. His nationwide search for Scarlett was nothing more than a publicity stunt but succeeded in getting the United States hyped up about the movie. He was already shooting the movie when he found the perfect woman to play Scarlett, Vivien Leigh. The British actress was in Hollywood to visit her boyfriend, Laurence Olivier, and also to land the role of Scarlett—and not in that order, either. Leigh had read the book several times and *knew* she would be perfect. She was right.

AFTERMATH

Gone With the Wind won an unprecedented ten Oscars and was the biggest box-office success until *Star Wars*. After filming, Leigh and Gable got divorced from their respective mates and married their respective sweethearts, Laurence Olivier and Carole Lombard. A few years later Lombard died in a plane crash during her war bond effort. Leslie Howard also died in a crash when the plane he was traveling in was shot down by the German Luftwaffe in 1943.

254

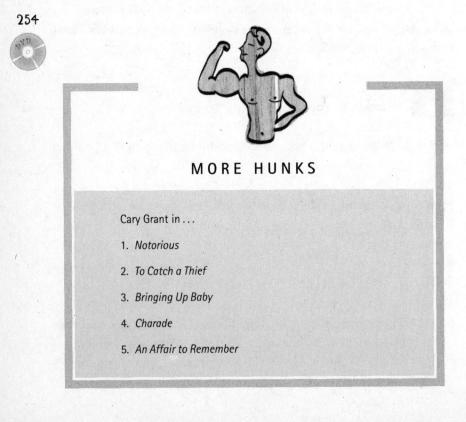

MORE HUNKS

Cary Grant in . . .

1. *Notorious*

2. *To Catch a Thief*

3. *Bringing Up Baby*

4. *Charade*

5. *An Affair to Remember*

The marriage of Vivien Leigh and Laurence Olivier ran into trouble, mostly due to her deteriorating mental health, as she suffered from what is now known as rapid cycling bipolar disorder. Poor Viv!

Ted Turner, who also suffers from a bipolar disorder, hails from Atlanta and named one of his sons Rhett. Turner spent over ten million dollars digitally remastering *Gone With the Wind* to restore it to its original glory.

Jules et Jim (1961)

Not rated

Directed by François Truffaut

Starring Jeanne Moreau, Oskar Werner, Henri Serre, Marie Dubois

THE PLOT

It is Paris, right before World War I. Two friends, Jules (Oskar Werner), an Austrian biologist, and Jim (Henri Serre), a French writer, meet a carefree woman named Catherine (Jeanne Moreau). Both men fall in love with her and she falls in love with both men. So begins the thirty-year love triangle, or as Truffaut called it, "a pure three-sided love." Didn't the French invent ménage a trois? Catherine marries Jules; the two men go off to fight on opposite sides in the war. After the war, Jim goes to visit Jules, Catherine, and their daughter. Jules cannot cope with his wife's restlessness and suggests that Jim marry her. At least this way they would all stay together.

Before there was *Two Guys and Girl*, before there was *Two Girls and a Guy* for that matter, there was *Jules et Jim*. If your daughters have an aversion to foreign films and subtitles, encourage them—bribe them, even—to get over it. If you don't, they may go through their lives without meeting one of our favorite goddesses, Jeanne Moreau. Do you want that on your conscience?

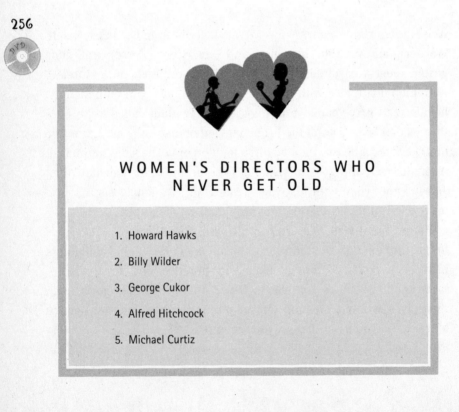

♥♥ *Bonding Potential: 6*

We love Catherine—she is a force of nature, unconventional and independent. And she's fun, too! In the beginning of the twentieth century, Catherine demands—and gets—the same freedom as a man. Jules and Jim try to understand her:

Jules: Do you approve of my wanting to marry Catherine? Tell me quite frankly.

Jim: I wonder if she is really made for having a husband and children. I am afraid she will never be happy on this earth. She is an apparition for all to appreciate, perhaps, but not a woman for any one man.

256

WOMEN'S DIRECTORS WHO NEVER GET OLD

1. Howard Hawks

2. Billy Wilder

3. George Cukor

4. Alfred Hitchcock

5. Michael Curtiz

Hunk Factor: 0

As much as we love men who love women, these guys are not for us.

 Hankie Factor: 2

As Truffaut put it, "Women cry, a lot of men get pissed off."

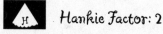 Squirming in Your Seat Watching a Sex Scene with Your Mother/Daughter Factor: 0

BEHIND THE SCENES

257

When Jeanne recited a line of dialogue, "Would someone here be willing to scratch my back?" a prop man bounded on the set, ready to do just that, so natural was her delivery.

AFTERMATH

Intellectuals see this movie as an allegory of Europe after World War I. Okay, if that's how they want it.

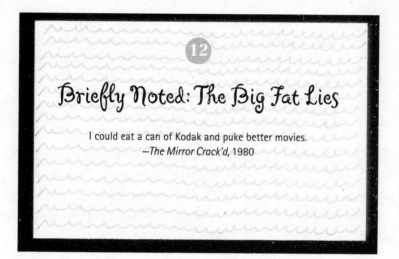

12

Briefly Noted: The Big Fat Lies

I could eat a can of Kodak and puke better movies.
—*The Mirror Crack'd*, 1980

The following movies are not fairy tales, fables, or fantasies—they are overblown, unrealistic, misleading fabrications that send the world the wrong message, and are insulting while doing it. In his autobiography *How to Talk Dirty and Influence People*, Lenny Bruce summed it up best when he said, "I learned there is no Judge Hardy, there is no Andrew, nobody has a mom like Fay Bainter. Oh, God, the movies really did screw us up."

The Best of Everything (1959)

So she won't become a hard-bitten career woman like Amanda Farrow (Joan Crawford) and wear her lipstick over the lipline, Caroline Bender (Hope Lange) ends up happily ever after with Steve (Stephen Boyd), the slacker in the office. Too bad Steve seems to be on the verge of acute alcohol poisoning. In his every scene, he is drunk or hungover. (He drinks on the job, too!) We get the message: Better to be with a sot than single.

Disclosure (1994)

They spend millions and millions of dollars making a movie about a man being sexually harassed by his boss. What is *wrong* with this picture?

Indecent Proposal (1993)

Robert Redford's a rich guy who offers a million dollars to sleep with Demi Moore. Problem is, she's married to Woody Harrelson and—oh, no!—Woody has gambled away all their dough. What's a girl to do?

P.S. Redford may be past his prime but, really, we're not talking Jeffrey Tambor here. He still looks like Robert Redford.

Flashdance (1983)

This plot is about as believable as *Frankenstein Meets the Killer Devil Fish.*

Love with the Proper Stranger (1963)

A girl who looks like Natalie Wood gets pregnant from a one-night stand with a sax player who looks like Steve McQueen. Time passes, her stomach stays flat, and Steve gives up his wastrel ways and falls in love with her. They marry. Yeah, right.

Maid in Manhattan (2002)

Do Hispanic chambermaids from the Bronx usually have romances with high-Wasp candidates for the U.S. Senate? If so, why would they? Watch *Cinderella* instead—it's more realistic. (There's a scene where talented actors Ralph Fiennes and Stanley Tucci make "ass/asset" puns. Guys—do you need money that badly?)

Pretty Woman (1990)

Have you ever seen a hooker who looks like Julia Roberts? No? In fact, have you ever seen a hooker who wasn't strung out on drugs? No? Ever seen a john as handsome and nice as Richard Gere? No? Well, you never will either.

Seven Brides for Seven Brothers (1954)

Young girls find love and happiness and marriage after being kidnapped by a pack of YY chromosome brothers. Do the cute brides find love and happiness and inbreeding with a pack of Hatfield-McCoy rejects? You bet!

Splendor in the Grass (1961)

It's not easy breaking up with your boyfriend when you're in high school. But does it really require a ten-year stint in the loony bin? We join those folks who call this movie "Splinter Up Your Ass."

Striptease (1996)

Poor Demi. (Again.) Now, she's a struggling single mom who loses her job. What choice had she, really, than to take a job as a stripper at the Eager Beaver? This means she's forced to show her body off and we know how much Demi hates *that*.

That Touch of Mink (1962)

Stinks. If *you're* on your way to work and a chauffeur-driven limo splashes you, ruining your outfit, the limo will keep on driving. Every time. The rich guy in the backseat will *not* chase you down, he will *not* get you a replacement wardrobe, and he will *not* look like Cary

Grant. In fact, he will probably look more like Danny DeVito with big tufts of hair in his ears.

An Unmarried Woman (1978)

If you've just been dumped by your husband for a younger woman, have a crabby teenage daughter and no career, it's safe to say you probably won't immediately find a handsome, sensitive, successful artist who wants to spend the rest of his life with you. Especially if your nose keeps running all the time like Jill Clayburgh's does.

Any Woody Allen movie

Any of the Woody Allen movies where beautiful young women—Julia Roberts, Elizabeth Shue, Drew Barrymore, Helen Hunt—fall in love with and lust after Woody. Isn't that *all* of his movies? We want to propose a movie where Colin Farrell, George Clooney, and Tobey Maguire all fall in love with and lust after Shirley MacLaine.

Index

265

269

270